Miracle Moments in Travel

Experiencing God's Love on the Road

Shannon Robak
with Contributing Authors

AUTHORPRENEUR
ACADEMY

Also available at Amazon.com
Paperback, Kindle, Nook, iBooks, and .pdf

ISBN-13: 978-0-9904403-9-0
ISBN-10: 0-9904403-9-7

Authorpreneur Academy, LLC.

www.Authorpreneur-Academy.com
info@authorpreneur-academy.com

Contents

vi   *Acknowledgments*

vii   *Introduction*

1   **African Safari** - Shannon Pogodzinski

5   **Sometimes All You Can Do Is Pray** - Mary Pergiovanni

13   **Mile High Miracle** - Katelyn Hutchison

15   **God Abroad** - Sarah Sinsky and Andrea Janota

19   **Let Go and Let God** - Corey Klein

27   **My Journey with God on the Road to Recovery** - Katie LaBlanc

31   **God is Alive and Well in Kathmandu, Nepal** - Doreen Robak

37   **Plans for Me** - Wanda Lucas

43   **Jesus Takes the Wheel** - Courtney Mulica

49   **Butterfly by My Side** - Devon Liebl

53   **God Loves You** - Tiffany Robak

61   **A Walk with a Stranger** - Allison Alexander

65   **Japanese Butterflies** - Shannon Robak

70   *A Note About "Miracle Moments in Travel"*

71   *About the Author*

We will tell the next generation the praiseworthy deeds of the Lord, His power, and the wonders He has done.

Psalm 78:4

This book is dedicated to God and His angels.

*Thank you for traveling with us
wherever we go.*

Acknowledgments

Thank you to all of the women who contributed to the creation of this book. Your insightful reflections on potentially difficult topics does not go unnoticed; thank you for venturing out of your comfort zone and for finding the courage and strength to share your story. Without your bravery in putting words to the pages, we wouldn't have a book!

It's easy to see that the stories that fill the pages to come are written from the heart. I hope you enjoyed the journey of the writing process and were able to discover untapped parts of yourselves. Thank you for taking the time to sit down and write - we all know that is not easy! Most importantly, thank you for putting up with me! May God's blessings continue to pour down on you and your families and may you continue to feel His presence.

I also would like to thank my brother, Lukey, for being such a great motivator and for always encouraging me. Thank you for being so patient and for taking the time to explain things over and over again. In teaching yourself to publish books, you make it possible for many people to share their voices with the world.

Introduction

If you knew God was with you wherever you went, would you travel more? Would you feel more at peace knowing that you were constantly held in His loving care?

In the following pages, 14 women share their *Miracle Moments in Travel*. Each woman's story is unique; each with her own creative writing style. However, all of our experiences share a common theme - the most loyal travel companion is God, and only He can change our hearts. Not only does God lead us and guide us to where we are meant to be, He travels alongside us as well.

From the churches in Ireland, to the mountains of Italy, to the roads in America, God is always with us and makes His presence known, reminding us that we are exactly where we are meant to be. God has already decided the path for each of us and He loves us more than we can possibly imagine. No matter our circumstances or where we go, God will never abandon us.

Through faith, the power of prayer, and His grace, it is remarkable to see what God has done in our lives. Our hearts have been filled with an indescribable joy and we did our best to share that with you.

This book was created because God has blessed our lives in incredible ways. It is the least we can do to thank God for giving us these wonderful opportunities. Our experiences are meant to be shared with you...they are too glorious to hide. We hope our stories will give you hope, inspire you to travel, and most importantly bring you closer to God. Happy reading and happy traveling!

African Safari

By: Shannon Pogodzinski

It's a Thursday night in February. I have three foot long subs in tow, and I'm stopping over at my Grandparents house for dinner, just before I head out of the country for a three week African safari. It's cold, I've just started a new job, and my spirits are a bit low. I know this will warm my heart and rejuvenate my spirit in a way not much else can.

After we eat, Grandma is busy around the kitchen and I sit with Grandpa in the living room, he in his chair and me on the couch. Where we always sit when we are together there.

Grandpa is asking about my trip, and telling me how he loved to travel and about his time in Germany during the war. He gives me $10 to buy a hamburger, like he always does. I say I will, like I always do (even though I've been a vegetarian for years now, a concept that is not well understood by Grandma and Grandpa.)

As I leave, I pause under the porch light and think about how lucky they are to love each other as much as they do, and how lucky I am to have that love (and them) in my life.

I arrive in Africa, waiting for the moment I can log into my email. Not something I'd typically do after travelling to another continent for an adventure, and a fresh perspective. But, Grandpa had unexpectedly gone into the hospital the day before I left, and I wanted to hear he was doing ok. For two days, I heard nothing. In this case, I knew that no news was not good news. I knew everyone was avoiding me, not because they didn't want to hear the glorious details of the trip, but because they knew I'd be on the next plane home if something had happened.

I pleaded for someone to email me and tell me how things were going. I reassured them I could handle it. And then, the next morning, the email came. Grandpa was gone.

Time stood still. I didn't know what to do. What I should do. I felt frozen. What does one do when they get this kind of news, and hundreds of thousands of miles separate you from running to the people you need to be with?

It was raining, but I needed to get out of that room. I needed to do something. So, I walked. Aimlessly at first. I found the ocean. Rain was pouring, the sea was roaring, meeting the grey clouds and sky somewhere on the horizon.

I was so, so far away, I wanted to go home. My parents and family had told me not to. It was a condition of their email. They said he wouldn't want me to. And actually, I knew that was true.

I stayed there by the sea for a long while. Just staring, standing, praying, disbelieving, yet believing and trying to make sense.

I went back to the room. I knew I needed to face my travel comrades eventually. I showered, I got ready. I'm not sure how I went through these motions. It was all so surreal. Here I am, on the other side of the world, my family is at home grieving, my grandpa is no longer here. I didn't get to say goodbye. But in a way, I did. I didn't know it yet, but I was luckier than most to have those final moments with him.

We decided to walk down to the marina, it had stopped raining and looked like it may clear up. The sun came out, warmth hit my shoulders, and against the backdrop of the ocean, I felt...ok. Heartbroken at my core, but I was functioning. I was moving. I wasn't in the fetal position. I was not inconsolably sobbing. I was at least able to acknowledge that this was good. Maybe even impressive. We arrived at the harbor, found some wine and I could converse (Again, noting, this is good. Maybe even again, impressive.) We even celebrated, him. We toasted, to him.

The next few days were a blur, but based on the nature of this trip – there was a lot of moving around, and travel time, which allowed me to be alone with my thoughts and grieve in my own way.

Daily, I found myself staring out my window seat, watching as we passed over clouds and sunsets, tears streaming down my face. I'm not sure where or when, but at some point, in a jeep, the warm sun on my face, as we were no doubt chasing the elusive leopard, I realized I was meant to be here. Quite literally, I was meant to be here. The sun and the clouds, the birds, everything seemed to have the spirit and presence of my Grandpa. I knew he was with me. I could feel him and see him everywhere I looked. He was there with me that day on the beach.

I realized then, God knew me. I would have been a mess back home. Probably inconsolable. Probably unable to function. Probably scared of my own grief and sadness. Probably, more or less, a burden to those who needed me more than I should have needed them. God had put me in this place, literally across the globe, so I could grieve. So I could see, and learn from my own strength.

So I could feel the warmth of the sun, see the beauty of the sky, and be reminded of both Grandpa's and God's presence in my life. This whole situation again reminded me, at the grandest level, there are no such things as coincidences. Everything happens for a reason. God will provide for you, and give you what you need, when you need it, even if you don't, or can't, realize it at the time.

Fast forward to the last night of the trip. I had been agonizing over how to spend the last $10 Grandpa will have ever given me. What could I possibly buy that would put this money to good use? Be meaningful? Special? Town after town, market after market, I'd been searching high and low for something to jump out and say "this is it."

Then that last night it hits me. I will buy a hamburger. So on the last night of our journey, overlooking a beautiful watering hole, as the sun was setting across an African plain, I ate a hamburger on Grandpa.

Sometimes All You Can Do Is Pray

By: Mary Pergiovanni

When patients are seated in my dental chair, they kindly inquire how I'm doing. And more than a few ask, "Are you going again this year....?" I thank them for asking, and say "yes," because right now two friends and I are overseeing a year-round medical clinic in Honduras. "October," I say. They nod, sit back and usually it's time to talk about their teeth at this point--and that's pretty much the conversation. A few people have asked more about the clinic, or other trips I've been on to other countries; but ultimately, I know many find it hard to understand how people live-and suffer-in the rest of the world.

It never fails to amaze me how much I have in terms of material wealth, compared to most of the people I visit. I have three meals a day any time I want, and a Dunkin' Donuts card. A car. A roof over my head. Clean water. Well-stocked kitchen cabinets, with food and yes, cans of Slim-Fast. What a blessing to live in America. I want to kiss the ground each time I get back. Seriously.

I'll give you a little background about where my traveling comes from.

In the 60's, my parents subscribed to Reader's Digest Condensed Books, which I loved; and one book made a big impression on me. "The Good Ship Hope" detailed the voyages of a hospital ship which enabled medical teams to perform life-saving surgery in third-world countries. That was always in the back of my mind, especially in the days of the Peace Corps, and I became very interested in things medical. Years later, in the 70's, I became a registered nurse, and then ultimately went to dental school in the 80's. I discovered that my oral surgery professor was the son of missionary parents and that he and his wife had done mission work in India. He was very active in an organization that sponsored one and two-week trips to foreign countries to help the poor. This information found a secure place in my heart next to "The Good Ship Hope." Maybe someday.

I graduated from Dental School in 1983 and worked in a general dental practice with my husband, and then the recession of the late 80's hit. Here in Connecticut, we were fairly sheltered from the effects; we did not see people with signs that said, "WILL WORK FOR FOOD," which were more common in the South. I was insulated, for sure. However, we happened to take a trip to Washington D.C. and that changed everything for me. We had breakfast in an upscale hotel and I was flabbergasted to pay $16.00 for a cup of coffee and an English muffin. (I still think in terms of my first weekly paycheck of $64 a week.) Outrageous! While still in this frame of mind, upon exiting the hotel, I just about tripped over a man trying to keep warm on a grate in the sidewalk, with his sign begging for a job. That did it for me. Everyone has these moments where something makes them stop dead in their tracks, and they know that they have to "Do Something."

My "Do Something" finally gelled and made me look up my old professor to find out more about mission trips. He arranged for me to go on a two-week mission trip to Jamaica. He knew several of the folks going on that one, and knew they would look out for me.

This was a life-changing experience. Away from the resorts that ringed the beautiful beaches, we saw many who lived in incredible poverty. We rode on a bus for hours to the interior of the country, and while driving in the dark, I saw no electric lights; just occasional fires illuminating people moving ghostlike on the roads. Their dwellings were huts made of sheet metal, tree branches, and plastic sheets. I seriously wondered what I had gotten myself into. There were no telephones for at least twenty miles. We communicated with the outside world via ham radio; each night some of the docs would send an antenna up a palm tree and start the process of locating a ham who could patch us through.

We stayed in a basic "camp" that had running water and toilets; and the high-ceilinged cinderblock rooms had bunks where 20-30 people could sleep. What I didn't know was that the water that came out the faucets was collected in an open barrel on the roof. 'Runny belly', the local term for diarrhea and fever, soon followed for many of us. Creatures-mainly lizards, spiders, and feral dogs, had the run of the place.

Each day we set out to different areas, and people came from miles around to have their aching teeth extracted. "Poor" didn't describe them--they were beyond poor. I asked parents, "How many children do you have?" -a usual conversation starter at home. "I had six, but lost three." "I had eight but lost two." "I lost four." My God, how was this possible? I had absolutely no idea. "Child mortality" was not some vague statistic when you actually spoke to these mothers. I learned to stop asking about the children. To say I was a naive American was an understatement.

The work I was doing was very different than what I did at home. Something that really bothered me was to take permanent teeth, especially the front teeth, out of children as young as 7 or 8 years. We had no way to fix them, and they were actually too far gone to save. I felt that I was mutilating them. Due to their poor diet and poverty, they went into the fields and ate sugar cane.

Without toothbrushes, their teeth were doomed, for sure. But in the big picture, teeth were the least of their problems. However, we did what we could to relieve people of their pain.

One evening, we were asked by the camp cook if we would be able to treat some of the workers in the laundry building. It was pitch dark, there was no electricity. All we had were headlamps. The laundry building contained huge sinks filled with water and soaking sheets. We threaded our way between lines of laundry. I recognized some of the kitchen helpers and drivers. They patiently, humbly, waited their turn while we took out their teeth in the darkness. They were too shy to approach us during the day. It felt like the Twilight Zone.

One day I was asked to go by myself to a location so that they could split up the dental teams in order to see more people. Upon arriving, there was already a huge crowd of people outside the tiny clinic building. At midday it became clear to the dozens of people that I would not be able to treat them all, and the mood quickly got really ugly. They started shouting at each other in the little waiting room and outside in the yard. Someone outside had a knife and threatened the huge lady, Joy, who ran the clinic. She gave it right back to him-"I know where you live! I will get you!" Whoa!

After seeing 35 people that day, I was finally finished. My hands hurt too much to continue. Those were the most difficult extractions I'd ever had; and I have heard similar stories from other dentists about working in Jamaica. I felt terrible because it seemed that all I had succeeded in doing that day was basically helping only a "lucky few" and riling up the rest of the village.

On that trip I saw a clinic room that had an infant's incubator in it. There wasn't even a place to plug it in, since there was no electricity in the building. It looked like it had never been used after it arrived in the country. To top it off, there was a huge spider who had made himself at home in it. It was kind of a metaphor for a really broken, almost non-existent, health care system. There were 144,000 people in that section of the country, and only one dentist and a few doctors were normally available. We all felt so helpless for them.

The medical people on our trip had some pretty amazing stories, which we would share when everyone regrouped for the night. They worked in a tiny local hospital and were doing two cases at once in the OR in order to see as many people as possible, which is just unheard of here in this country. The nurses told me that chickens and cats were in the recovery rooms. They had one roll of adhesive tape in the whole place.

One night the medical team came back to camp really dispirited. They had tried to treat a woman with an emergency who ultimately did not survive, for lack of equipment readily available at any small hospital in the States. It turned out that she had developed a seriously irregular heartbeat. She needed to be cardioverted--to have the defibrillator with the paddles applied to her chest. But the machine at the hospital was a very old model and did not have a device called a synchronizer. They would not be able to time the charge at the proper time in her heartbeat, and they felt so helpless as they told the family they could do nothing.

The family was devastated; but they told the docs that they were very grateful for all that they had tried to do for her. They asked God to bless the medical team that had come so far to help their people. Although the mood of the team was subdued for the rest of the week, many shared how much it meant to them that the family consoled THEM with their prayers. The Jamaican people were in such dire need, but they still thanked God for what the American doctors had provided to many through life-changing surgery.

Finally, it came time to go home. It had been such a tough couple of weeks for so many reasons. Once I got home, I selfishly hoped that the poor people and the horrible conditions they lived in would not be so immediate--but my body seemed to remember every sad person, and the mothers telling me of the children who died. For weeks I couldn't eat. I had a terrible pain in my stomach and finally a doctor diagnosed an ulcer. Here I had tried to 'do something,' but it didn't feel like I had done anything at all...maybe only helped a few folks. All I could think of was, where was the Big Guy in all of this? How did people live like this? For such a big group to go there, what did we accomplish-talk about "rearranging the deck chairs on the Titanic"!

It took a long time for the stomach pain to go away. Although I still wanted to help, it took 5 years for me to attempt another trip.

In 1995, my grandmother passed away. She was an amazing woman, a tireless worker in the family restaurant, and had a genuine love of people. She told me how, as one of the few who did not get influenza during the epidemic in 1917, she was given a needle and anti-flu medicine and sent on her way to inoculate the people in her area. I can picture that 17-year-old trudging up and down mountains to reach the poor, tiny villages in Northern Italy. She later told me that she used the same needle on everyone though, and she felt she might have done more harm than good, but that's all they had. She was always very supportive of me, and to honor her memory and spirit I signed up for another trip, this time to the Dominican Republic.

This was a much smaller group. We prayed together in the morning for the people we were going to see. We had devotions at night, again with our patients in mind. This time was not so much of a culture shock for me; and I feel that the living conditions for the people were not as dire. We had a lot more help, and even though the work day was just as long and hot as it had been in Jamaica, it was a totally different experience.

Patty, a woman from North Carolina, volunteered to be my helper. We got to talking about birthdays, and hers was the same date as when my grandmother passed away. I felt then that this was a direct sign from both the Big Guy and my grandmother! Grandma had talked about ways she was going to "get in touch with me" after she had passed, and this made me smile (I also remembered a priest saying that "as far as God is concerned, there are no "coincidences." I do love a good coincidence.)

So, I was secretly tremendously pleased by this date "sign," purely coincidental though the average person might think it was. I ventured to ask Patty about me sharing it with the group that evening during devotions. "What do you think?" I asked. I still laugh to this day when I remember her honest answer: "They'll think you're out of your m-i-i-i-nd." So I kept that little tidbit to myself.

I felt more connected to the patients, and felt that I was able to help a lot more since I was able to fix teeth and not just pull them out. I still remember the amazement and pleasure on the faces of the parents of a 10-year-old girl when she returned to them with her teeth restored. They had expected her to be missing several in the front, as they were all heavily decayed (thanks to sugar cane.) The girl herself was beaming when I showed her that her teeth were all fixed, like new. Even though on short-term mission trips we stay in country only a week or two and then leave, I liked to imagine that for this particular girl, her self-esteem was preserved. Taking that thought a bit further: maybe she was able to do better in school, found a better job, and maybe she did not feel self-conscious in her interactions with others.

I don't have any deep thoughts about why the first trip was so hard, and why the second trip paved the way for 32 subsequent trips to the Dominican Republic, Mexico, Ecuador, Haiti, and especially Honduras, where most of my time has been spent. I wouldn't dare to presume that God was speaking directly to me about anything in particular. But I felt that maybe there was a reason things worked out the way they did. There were many things that I had been taught as a child and had filed away, which only later, on these trips, made total sense.

There's an old joke: "What's the difference between praying in church and praying at the casino?" Answer: "At the casino you REALLY mean it!!!!" I have to laugh. OMG, do I pray when I'm on these trips! (Aside from my usual prayers for a safe landing, protection from "runny belly", and safety while navigating in countries that have government travel warnings.)

I pray we do not harm our patients because of any unknown medical conditions. Many people have the same issues that you find here in the States, only in their country they are undiagnosed, or they might not be able to afford medicine.

Many times they have walked hours to be seen; often they have not eaten for a day. It's very hot, they are tired, and they are fragile. We have taken to providing little snacks like crackers, cookies, and water, so that people don't pass out during procedures, especially after waiting all day. With almost every person, they put the snack in their pocket instead of eating it; whether it is for "later" or for their family members at home who have little food is hard to know, but it always breaks my heart. We have to insist that they eat it first.

With each patient, I am "really praying" (like I do at the casino...) Sometimes the prayer is more like, "OMG....OMG....OMG...." In a poor country there are no safety nets like we are used to at home. We have no x-rays, so sometimes we start something and it's like opening Pandora's Box. On my second trip I asked a local M.D. if there was anything like being able to call 911. Did they have an ambulance and paramedics? Now this place was in the back of beyond, tiny--the animal population far outnumbered the people--and it was dirt poor. To answer my serious question, the doctor just put his head back and laughed out loud until I kind of slunk off.

One thing I am always sure of--I know the people back home are praying for us while on these trips. They will never know how much that means to me personally; how empowering that is. I imagine that their prayers follow and surround us. I can ask for some of these prayers to protect each person I see--like taking money out of a bank, in case my own prayers aren't good enough. Theologically speaking, not very sophisticated, but over the years it has gradually become a way of thinking that helps. I do feel that God is watching over the work and over us. My oral surgery teacher once told me on a trip we took together: "It's like you are looking at a parade through a knothole in a fence. You only see part of it. God sees the whole thing. He understands." That made so much sense to me.

There have been many times that I have seen very moving, memorable things. On one trip I spent some time watching one of our physicians as he examined patients. Although he didn't speak their language, his calm, gentle demeanor was so soothing to them. After he gave them their prescriptions to fill at our pharmacy, he asked if he could pray with them. They sat quietly with closed eyes and bowed heads, and he took their hands and prayed that God would give them better health, and bless their families. There was such a feeling of peace that settled over all. Here in a tiny, quiet corner, amid the sounds of the bustling clinic, people coming and going, dogs wandering in and out, I was witnessing such a miracle: God was with us. I have that picture forever etched in my memory - "Wherever two or three are gathered in My name, there I am with them."

One of the great things about going on a mission trip is that we get to run our clinics with local people who lead us, take care of us, and help us take care of our patients. The majority of people in these countries that we have tried to help are so incredibly poor in terms of material things, but so kind-hearted, so appreciative.

It's happened that we could not treat people even after they waited all day. We would ask them to come back early the next day and they were so understanding. It was never a problem. There was another time we had packed everything up and the clinic was finished. Our supplies were already on the truck. Some new people came in seeking treatment, and we had to apologize. One lady said, "Don't worry, I will wait for the next team; they are coming in three months. God bless you for helping us."

Many times patients have come back to the clinic with little tokens of affection that they made or bought--a picture, a homemade card, a keychain, a plastic flower. Sometimes they would come by with some tortillas, or tiny cups of hot coffee to share with as many of us as possible. In spite of everything that life has handed them--homes lost in mudslides; poverty and malnutrition, low life expectancy for them and their children, they are so genuine, so warm-hearted.

I have gone to Mass with them--the Mass in Honduras is a good two hours long, as opposed to 45 minutes or so here in the States--and witnessed lots of heartfelt singing and praying. A sermon approaching an hour in length is the norm, but the people follow it intently.

One time I wondered aloud what exactly they might be praying for, compared to what people in America might pray for. Al, a dentist friend with me, suggested that maybe they were "praying for life to be a little less hard."

Suddenly so much made sense, after so many trips. His words have always stayed with me. It is such a beautiful, simple answer. I realized then that maybe our mission groups really couldn't make any differences in the overall big picture. But maybe, even though we couldn't stay too long, we could do our best for each person--to make their lives "a little less hard." I like to think that, with God's help, that is what we are able to do.

Mile High Miracle

By: Katelyn Hutchison

Fear, panic and anxiety all make it difficult for me to travel. There are many opportunities that I have missed out on, simply because I have a fear of flying. For example, take the time I was all set to travel to Breckenridge, Colorado for a weekend of skiing with my good friends from college. I wish this was a story about a miracle I witnessed in the mountains that weekend. Unfortunately that is not the case. Fear overtook me and I never made it to Colorado.

Let me give you a little recap of what happened that morning. I had an early morning flight scheduled and so we left the house before sunrise while the sky was still dark. As soon as we turned onto the main road, both front headlights of the car burned out and so we had to turn around to switch cars. I was thinking this was definitely a sign that I should stay home, but we drove to the airport anyway. I was already feeling uneasy prior to our mishap and now we were running late. I couldn't shake my fear.

My husband dropped me off at the airport and I eventually made it to my gate. There I sat alone, stomach hurting, sweat dripping, and heart pounding. The flight attendant announced, "Last call for Denver, Colorado." I never got on the plane. I went home extremely upset knowing that I would be missing out on a great weekend with friends. There have been numerous missed opportunities just like this one because of my fear of flying.

However, I have also met some wonderful people who have crossed my path at just the right time to help ease my fears. You can call it coincidence if you want, but I strongly believe these individuals were meant to be sitting near to me to help me in moments of anxiety. The first such encounter happened on a trip to New York City. I was looking forward to an extended Mother-Daughter weekend with two of my college roommates and our moms. However, I had of course spent the majority of the weeks before the trip worrying about the flight.

The day of the trip finally arrived and as expected, I was feeling anxious. The time quickly came to board the plane. I gathered my carry on, held tight the worry stone in my pocket, and prayed for a safe flight as we walked through the gate.

I took my seat and soon found myself starting to panic. I teach first grade and so I reached into my bag and took out some papers to grade. I thought this might distract me from the worry that I knew was about to overtake me. As I was about to put my headphones on, also meant to help distract me, a woman sat down next to me and said, "Do you teach special ed?" This led into a discussion about her son, while we watched the standard safety video. From there we talked and talked and I learned what seemed to be every detail of that woman's life.

The next thing I knew we were circling over New York City as the weather was keeping us from landing. It didn't even bother me that we were slightly delayed and spent more time in the air than originally planned. It was a miracle.

The entire plane ride I hadn't thought about my fear of flying and wasn't worried or panicked at all. I even peaked out the window to take in the sights of New York from above. This is no small feat for someone who typically spends flights glued to their seat afraid to look anywhere but straight ahead! When we landed and were about to exit the plane, I leaned over to the woman, thanked her, and told her that I believed she was put on this plane to help me get through the flight. She agreed!

I encountered another similar experience on my flight home from Italy. Prior to this trip, I had actually been prescribed medicine to help calm my nerves. However, this flight seemed to be especially bumpy which was not helping matters at all. I was sitting next to my sister, but in this type of situation, it is difficult, if not impossible to calm me down.

I then noticed a man and woman next to me. The woman seemed just as afraid, if not more than I was. The man was consoling her and noticed that I too, was not enjoying the flight. He then leaned over to try and comfort me by saying, "It's okay- we are just going through clouds." Throughout the flight he continued to reassure me, and his travel companion, that everything was fine. He did not have to do this, but he did. He was able to calm me down, and as mentioned before, that is not an easy task.

Although it may not seem like much, each of these experiences has made traveling easier for me. Each flight was full of hundreds of people and I could have been sitting next to any of them. But my seat just happened to be next to the individuals that helped me tremendously throughout the flights. God knew what He needed to do to get me through these flights; and for that I am forever grateful.

God Abroad

By: Sarah Sinsky and Andrea Janota

My story of experiencing miracles in travel begins on the bank of Lake Garda in the small town of Riva del Garda, Italy. I was visiting the holiday destination with Pietro, a good friend while studying abroad. Sitting on that bank, taking in the clean fresh air, gorgeous mountains, and different cultures around me, I realized I was in the presence of God. I had realized this many times prior, but nature always reminded me that the world was a much larger place than me, that I was a servant living in the huge world God created. For me, nature was the place I felt most connected...and this setting happened to be the most connected I ever felt to God.

And while I would consider myself a consistently happy person, being in the presence of God in such a simple, yet profound way, brought out euphoria. It reminded me that true happiness, true miracles come from letting go of fear and trusting in God. Before I continue, I will start at the beginning.

Growing up in a large, Catholic family, faith was the most important thing. Finding strength and love through God and spirituality was the underlying value of my family. We gathered for holidays through God, food, and togetherness. We celebrated one another's accomplishments and were there for one another through difficult challenges. Creating incredible relationships within my family was only possible due to our faith. We also have a strong Irish heritage...anyone who knows me is aware of the pride I possess in my Irish ancestry. This love for family, Irish heritage, and my strong faith led me to a desire to study abroad.

Fast forward to the beginning of college, and although I was an undeclared major I knew I wanted to study abroad. I saw studying abroad not only as a way to better understand various cultures, but grow closer to God through learning about people not similar to me. I also saw the chance to go abroad as a way to grow closer to familial ties by studying in Ireland. After switching majors twice in my freshman year and many meetings with advisors, I found a way to study abroad! The fact that my dream of many years would come true was exciting. What I did not expect was the fear associated.

Once I knew I would be going abroad, the sense of fear came from nowhere and was unexpected. I spent so much time in excitement and planning that living in a foreign country for four months terrified me. Many questions came to mind...how would I do in a different country? How would I do meeting new people and traveling alone? How do I pay for all the trips I want to take? All these thoughts turned into a frozen rush of panic and anxiety. I prayed heavily prior to leaving for Ireland and decided to let go of the fear to trust God.

Letting go of the fear allowed for me to embrace all experiences while abroad. I took classes at an Irish university, explored Irish villages and learned quickly the importance of being part of a community. I made a great group of friends and learned more about my family, which brought me closer to God.

I also learned a great deal about myself. I never thought traveling alone to be something I would consider or enjoy, as I love the company of others. Yet when friends in Ireland were unable to come with me on a week trip of Europe, I decided to go alone and meet friends from other countries along the way. The thrill of planning trip itineraries was electrifying, but even more exhilarating was reminding myself to trust God and trust where He wanted me to explore when traveling. This trust led me to the most freeing and adventurous part of my trip, exploring northern Italy.

This trip began with meeting Pete in Rome. It was 5:30 in the morning and we were about to embark on a day long trip to Lake Garda. While Pete was fluent in Italian and I had done a great deal of planning, neither of us really knew where we were going. After two trains, a bus, and a nice Italian couple telling us when we needed to get off, we had made it to the southern shore of Lake Garda. A half hour later and realizing the hostel we booked was on the opposite end of the lake, we boarded another bus praying and trusting in God that he would lead us to where we were meant to be. Two hours and about 25 stops later we made it to our hostel.

We woke the next day with clear hearts and strong desires to explore the beautiful landscape and culture in which we ventured. The night before we had seen a bright light highlighting a small structure on top of the Italian Alps, and decided this was where we would hike to that morning. While neither of us brought appropriate hiking clothes or shoes, or really had any idea what we were getting into, the curiosity of the structure was too much to pass up. We began our climb and while several people passed us in athletic attire and walking sticks, the trust in God kept us going. I was grateful to Pete for telling me we were close to the structure even when we were not, and he was grateful I brought snacks. We truly relied on one another and felt the presence of God.

Two hours from the bottom of the mountain, exhausted and sunburned, we finally reached the structure built into the mountain. There, under a small, white wooden chapel, was a statue of Mary and an altar. I felt a rush of emotion and awe as I prayed in front of the altar and signed the prayer book in front of the statue. People from all over the world had signed this book, had ventured to this spot for a chance to experience God in a surreal way. Pete and I sat on a ledge in front of the chapel for about an hour, not only amazed by this little chapel, but by the incredible view of Lake Garda and the mountains surrounding us. For the first time in a long time, I felt I was surrounded by a miracle of God...that all the hard work and trust in Him to free myself from fear was worth it for this moment of complete awe. The beauty and feeling of being so small in such a large world was one I will never forget; sitting in shock of what God created in front of me was such a gift. I never would have found this miracle of a place if I had not let go and let God be such a presence in my life.

For many people, traveling is done with reason, plans, and some kind of mission. While my traveling abroad started out as this, it led me to the miracles God has created through cultures unknown to me and landscapes I could not comprehend. I am grateful for growing up in a family of such strong culture and faith in God, which allowed me to further explore my own culture and faith. These adventures allowed me to explore joy in the most simple, pure ways...opening myself up to the possibilities of falling in love with people and cultures unknown.

A dear friend of mine, Andrea Janota, also studied abroad and expressed how her experience overseas also showed her miracles, or as she called them, her "God moments". This is her experience with miracles in traveling:

It is from the purest place of honesty that I say the time spent studying abroad in Quito, Ecuador was one of the most spiritual times of my life. I lived in Quito for a total of ten months and attended Pontificia Universidad Católica del Ecuador, a Catholic university in the heart of the country's capital city. The school was situated far in the mountains, with views of volcanoes lying dormant in the distance. I lived in the neighborhood of La Floresta with the most amazing family. I truly believe they were a blessing by Great design. Without their acceptance, love, and support, I'm not sure my ears would have been as open to the miracles that fell upon me. In my own experience, I called these "God moments." Years later, I still feel emboldened by their memory. I will share with you a few of my most powerful God moments in hopes that they will find resonance.

I arrived in Quito in August 2012 as a college junior. By October it was time to start thinking about returning stateside, planning classes to take in the spring semester. For me, it was also time to start prepping for the MCAT. Since high school, my only dream and ambition was to become a physician. To stay on the traditional trajectory towards medical school, I needed to take the MCAT during my spring semester and begin applications. I felt a pull to do nothing of the sort. I wanted to stay in Quito. I wanted to travel more, learn more, and connect more. My God moment came when I emailed my academic counselor and expressed to her I wanted to consider staying another semester abroad. She refuted the idea. Told me no. Normally, I think I would have listened. I would have known that this is the road to becoming a doctor, and that's what I've always wanted to do. I can remember going through my bedtime routine and feeling overcome, filled with both grace and empowerment. I felt the Divine let me know that I could choose. And not only that I could choose, but I could also be an advocate for myself. In the truest way, I felt a Holy guidance, a spirit of love that allowed me to decide and that my amazing, wonder-filled God would direct me, guide me, and give me the means to make things happen.

To this day, that is one of, if the not the most, defining moments of my journey. My lesson from God was reinforced as I went through the process of petitioning my college for permission to stay abroad. I made multitudes of requests to administrators. I was asked to argue my case and finagle my plans repeatedly. Then I stayed in Quito for another semester. I continued my pursuit of finding God in the biggest and loudest and tiniest and quietest of moments.

The first God moment I wanted to tell you about I received alone; it was my personal struggle of rebuking what I was told to do and figuring out what I was meant to do. The second I want to share, I found in fellowship. Although this time God used others to help deliver me a message, I saw how uniquely the Lord moves in each of our own lives individually. The lesson I found was not similar, and maybe even in stark contrast, to the ones He expressed to my peers. This God moment taught me to seize life, to make each experience what I want it to be. I turned to passages such as Ephesians 5:13-16 and phrases like " 'Wake up, O sleeper'...Be very careful, then, how you live--not as unwise, but as wise, making the most of every opportunity, because the days are evil."

These verses captivated me to love each day I spent walking through Quito, traveling to the coastal towns, hiking through the Andes, and to appreciate every person I was blessed enough to meet. I wanted to fight to make this experience the most rewarding it could possibly be. I learned this was not a real fight at all, but rather an embracing of myself and the awesome love our Lord has waiting for us. You can find the most unexpected and divine messages while traveling. I was emboldened by the Lord to be an advocate for myself, to steer my journey powerfully and gracefully, and squeeze every ounce of living out of each moment.

Let Go and Let God

By: Corey Klein

*"Do not fear, for I am with you; do not be dismayed, for I am your God. I will strengthen you, I will surely help you; I will hold you with my righteous strong hand." **(Isaiah 41:10)***

In May of 2013, I found myself back on a plane to visit my village, Salinas de San Vicente, Ecuador, about 10 months after finishing my Peace Corps service. In anticipation of attending graduate school that coming fall, I knew a return trip needed to happen sooner rather than later, so I excitedly spread the word to my Ecuadorian families of my upcoming visit, and off I went. To get to my village requires a five-hour bus ride; by the time my flight arrived, and I got myself to the bus terminal, I had a choice to spend the night and take a morning bus, or take the overnight bus and arrive earlier.

I had taken the same overnight bus ride countless times before during my 27-month service, so naturally I called my friend in Salinas to let her know to expect me around 6 am on the overnight bus. I brought Eckhart Tolle's book, *The Power of Now*, with me to read during this particular trip. Typically I cannot read on buses or in cars because I get nauseous, but I had been waiting for a chance to start this book. Not able to sleep with the humid air sticking to me, I cracked it open.

I felt my mind and body returning to the culture of Ecuador – slow down, throw away your to-do list, relax. Things will happen *ya mismo*, soon, when they're supposed to, God willing. He has everything under control. I was reading Chapter 5: The State of Presence, which reinforced this idea: be present, be still, be with God, who is the Divine Presence; be in the here and now. Don't worry about the future. I started to get sleepy, and nodded off while praying, reflecting on a desire to be more present, and thanking God for this opportunity to come back to my Peace Corps village sooner than I originally anticipated.

The roads in Ecuador are curvy. And bumpy. And fast. I woke to the feeling of the bus picking up speed. Ready to muster up my feisty Ecuadorian Spanish to yell at the bus driver to slow down, my vision became clear. He wasn't purposely speeding up, as the drivers tend to do when they want to race a bus from a competing company. Another man was standing next to him, holding a gun to his head, yelling at him to pick up the speed. *What? Is this real? Is this really happening right now?* I was still half-asleep, and I didn't want to believe we were in trouble.

We were forced to turn off the road, and the bus rocked back and forth more violently as it made a path through the tree branches and brush. This wasn't a real road! People around me woke up as well, startled by all the commotion. And then I saw them. The lights of the bus illuminated four other men, running towards us with their faces covered, weapons in hand: machetes, guns, and knives. *Oh dear God please help us.* This *was un asalto*, an assault, a robbery.

As quickly as I saw them outside of the bus, they were aboard and yelling obscenities. Fully awake and alert at this point, I grabbed my purse and threw it under the seat. Somehow I reacted quickly enough to hide it from sight of the hijackers. The woman next to me, seated in the window seat holding her baby, helped me kick the purse as close to the window as possible and out of view. Material things can be replaced, of course, but this purse contained my passport, ID, cards, cash, everything I would need to get back home in eight days. At this point I wasn't exactly looking forward to hanging out longer than planned.

My hands shot up in the air in an act of obedience. The men paced up and down the aisle, grabbing bags, jewelry, whatever they could find of value among the forty-some frightened passengers. I felt my heart racing, the tears welling in my eyes, and heard myself panic, "oh my God, oh my God." I started praying, praying, praying. And then something changed within me; the energy grew still, and I was no longer crying.

My breathing slowed, my mind and body covered in tranquility. I have no clue how my brain was functioning, but I remembered what I had just read, and the thoughts appeared: *be here, be still, God is with me.*

A man approached me, his pistol waving around in front of my face as he said, "Quítate los anillos." I quickly removed my two silver rings I wear each day. My pulse returned when he moved on to the next passenger. What happened next was a real blessing. The group of thieves, six in total, started arguing. One of them suggested they make everyone get off the bus. At the same moment, we could see lights passing by because we were close enough to the main road, not hidden very well by the surrounding trees. Spooked, another group member quickly shot down this idea and demanded that they leave right away.

To our surprise, that's exactly what they did. One by one, they filed out of the bus, and disappeared into the darkness.

No one appeared to be physically hurt, but we were shaken up, collectively taking a few minutes to gather ourselves. Once again, it appeared we were safe. *Thank You, thank You, thank You GOD.* One of the people near me said,

"You're the only foreigner on this bus, I'm surprised they didn't notice that. And please don't think our country is this way, Ecuadorians are very good people."

My mind raced – I'm glad they didn't notice I was a foreigner either! Who knows what would have happened had they realized; I didn't want to think about it. I explained to them my history with the country and reassured them that I know firsthand how beautiful, funny, and loving Ecuadorians are, and that difficult situations occur in every country, unfortunately.

Our bus was a mess, and in the process of traveling down the dirt road, we were now stuck. After some time we each were taken to a new bus stop and placed on other buses going the same route we had been heading on a few hours before. A very nice lady let me borrow her phone to call my friend. The time was close to 8 am by now; I wondered if she figured we were running late, which is not uncommon.

When I finally arrived at my village, she took me to her family's home where I was to stay for the next week. In true Ecuadorian fashion, news had spread quickly about what had happened.

Many told me that they had never experienced *un asalto* before. *Oh great, lucky me! People who have lived here and traveled throughout the country for decades have never had this happen, and I come back for a few days and this is how I'm welcomed back?!* They also informed me that we must have had amateur thieves.

Typically people are made to get off the bus, a truck comes (an accomplice) to load up the luggage stored underneath the bus, and usually people are forced to take off all of their clothes (more items to sell = more money). My mouth dropped open and my heart filled with more and more gratitude that things did not escalate to this point. *God is with me no matter what. He knows what He's doing.*

When I look back on my time in Ecuador, I still feel peace. I still feel this unique love that is unlike a love for any other place I've been. The rest of my visit with my Ecuadorian family was wonderful, similar to the time I spent with them during my service: mounds of rice, endless shrimp, bucket showers, sweat dripping down my back 24/7, afternoon soccer games, serving as a human jungle gym, weird smells, no alone time or personal space, hours sitting and talking with my friends, hearing the latest town gossip, entertaining comments about my weight, my inevitable marriage to an Ecuadorian man, and my riches from working for several months in the States.

All of this makes the experience what it is, a complex mix of love and wonder for a unique country. It was definitely where I was meant to be for that week, and of course for those years of service. How do I know this? You're about to find out.

I received my invitation to join Peace Corps Ecuador as a Youth Development Volunteer in early March of 2010. Ten days following receipt of my offer, I was to accept or decline the invitation to spend 27 months living and working somewhere in Ecuador. Ten days?! In my mind, I felt the tension building knowing how quickly a week and a half could fly by. I had to process all of this and make a decision, or lose out on a very competitive and unique opportunity. I had anxiously awaited the thick, bright blue envelope after attending a Q&A session in November of 2008, starting my application in January of 2009, sending it in that June, and sitting for an interview in July at the Milwaukee Public Library.

Needless to say I had been working through this process for a while. What entered my mind was unexpected. *Wow! I got an invitation! What do I do? Ecuador? This country was not even on my radar as a possibility. What do I know about this country? Some college friends studied abroad there. They rode donkeys. End of story. What am I thinking? I don't know what I'm doing. This is AWESOME! What an opportunity! Should I go? Or wait, maybe I should stay and keep working, you know, climb the ladder at work. Work? I mean, I like my job right now but not enough to think of doing it for the next 27 months! God please help me. Where do you want me to go? What am I supposed to do?*

At this point in my life, I had been working at La Causa - a non-profit, social services agency - for almost two years. Prior to graduation from St. Norbert College in 2008, La Causa was on my mind. I wasn't exactly sure why, but I had this strong feeling that La Causa was where my career was supposed to start. God was pointing me there very clearly.

I'm guessing most of us remember our first "real world, big kid" job: the nerves, the excitement, and the exhaustion that comes with creating a new normal. I enjoyed the families, adored my co-workers, and learned a great deal about the human services field. However, I felt completely overwhelmed. I experienced a high level of stress from engaging in emotionally-charged work, and didn't feel totally happy.

I worked a lot and couldn't seem to figure out when to work out, thus I felt more stressed from putting on a fresh chunk of LB's. Ok fine, the weekends spent drinking vodka-cranberries and devouring Qdoba burritos with the girls probably didn't help much either! I didn't feel like myself. I felt a little lost and unsure. I didn't know what I wanted to do, or if I was in the right place in my life. My relationship with God felt strained compared to when I was in college, or on service trips where I had felt His presence so strongly. Something needed to change.

I kept my Peace Corps invitation quiet from the world except for my family and a few close friends. Ever since the day I opened my offer letter in the mail, I felt distracted. My brain was spinning with thoughts. The clock ticked on and I felt nowhere near able to go back and check a box, yes or no, that would greatly alter my future. I prayed for God to send me some sort of sign to help me; muddling through the millions of positive and negative thoughts flying through my mind was confusing and noisy.

My parents suggested we meet up during that week for dinner at McCormick & Schmick's Seafood & Steaks at Mayfair Mall to talk more about the opportunity enclosed in the bright blue package. Of course we didn't go directly to the restaurant. I met my sister Kerstin and my mom in Macy's, and from there we walked through the mall for a bit while we waited for my dad to meet us. If you're familiar with Mayfair Mall, located soon after Macy's is J. Crew, and my mom wanted to stop in and take a look around. As we turned into the store, the first display contained some hats sitting on a long table; you couldn't miss them.

My mom gasped and smiled. "What?" I asked. She held up the small sign placed in front of the hats and showed it to me as she read aloud: "Panama hats. Hand-woven by women in Ecuador." My sister's big blue eyes grew even bigger as the three of us paused and looked at each other. "That's weird." We all blurted out almost in unison. I am not an avid J. Crew shopper, but I have never seen anything about Ecuador in a store, let alone there. In general, Ecuador is not a country you typically hear about, especially when you're looking for a fresh pair of Chinos to match your bright paisley cardigan.

We spent a few more minutes perusing the store and started to make our way out to meet my dad at the restaurant. My mom ran quickly to another store while Kerstin and I began walking back towards Macy's to exit the mall. Kerstin had asked me something about my thoughts on Peace Corps, and as I was about to answer, she interrupted:

"Ahhh look to your left" she awkwardly, nervously, half-chuckled as the words spilled out. I quickly looked over. I saw the biggest, most obvious sign I had ever seen. God definitely has a sense of humor when we're taking ourselves too seriously and not paying attention. In the big window front of Eddie Bauer was a sign. It read: "ADVENTURE ECUADOR!" painted in the window, accompanied with an outline of the country.

I looked back at Kerstin with my equally big eyes. We giggled in disbelief while also commenting, "Is that a sign or what?! Count that as sign number two!" *Okay God, I hear you. I'm listening.*

We sat down to dinner and began to tell my parents what had happened, and filled my dad in on J. Crew's Panama hats. We moved on to checking out the menus since none of us had been to this particular restaurant before. Being a Seafood restaurant, there was obviously a large list of fresh fish items for dinner. And well, well, well, whatta ya know, my dad started to read the very first item on this list: "a fresh fish from..." you guessed it, Ecuador. I believe at this point we were all just trying to keep up and started laughing. How was this happening?!

Okay God, I think I got the message. I think. Thank you.

I'm a big believer in signs, which is a huge reason why I asked God to smack me in the face with one. And he did just that, not once, but three times in the span of about an hour! Up until this point in my life, I had never received a message so loud and so clear. I knew that this was the path I was meant to take. I think my family knew it too. I did not know what awaited me, but I did know that God was right there with me, and in His time, according to His will, He would continue to reveal His plans for me. I learned so much within those few hours about letting go and giving all of my fears, hesitations, thoughts and struggles to God.

June 15, 2010 came within the blink of an eye; it was a sunny Tuesday morning, and it was the day I left for Ecuador. I tearfully said goodbye to my family and friends, and boarded a plane to Washington, D.C., for a three-day pre-service training, and then went on to Quito, Ecuador, with the 68 other volunteers who would serve with me. There's so much I could say about my experience, it's difficult to put it all into words. The pace of life slowed down, I felt able to become more present, more mindful, and be still in the presence of God more than I had in the States.

Early on in my service, my mother sent me a daily devotional book, *Jesus Calling*. This book was, and still is, an amazing, essential piece of my daily routine. This book facilitated a stronger relationship with God, an opportunity for intentional connection, to be fully present with Him each day. The culture of Ecuador also forced me to take time to be with others, to slow down and be still. I learned an incredible amount from the people in my village, from my cohort of fellow volunteers, and from other Ecuadorians.

Deciding to serve in the Peace Corps truly changed the trajectory of my life. Actually, I take that back. Deciding to serve in the Peace Corps was always God's plan; it was already woven into my story. He knows where we will end up; in my case, I needed some time to calm down, get quiet, practice patience, and trust, in order to understand and experience His plans unfolding.

Following Peace Corps, I spent a year working in Milwaukee while I applied to graduate school. Peace Corps has a couple different programs, one is Coverdell Fellows, for those who are interested in using their service towards gaining a graduate degree, and for universities who appreciate and welcome the skills that Returned Peace Corps Volunteers possess.

I had been contemplating going back to school since I started my application for Peace Corps; I knew I wanted to continue studies related to International Relations, Human Services, use my Spanish-speaking skills, etc., but had no idea if such a degree existed. Through my research on each of the Coverdell Fellows Universities, I discovered that my ideal graduate program indeed existed: it was a Master of Arts in International Disaster Psychology at the University of Denver, Colorado.

A combination of psychology, international studies, disaster and trauma relief, it truly encompassed several of my passions. Without Peace Corps, I am quite certain I would not have found such a fitting program for me in which to participate. There's no way my life would be what it is today, or that I would be the person I am today, without completing my service in Ecuador. God definitely prepared me for those two years, and for what has come after. In the right moment, according to His plan, in His timing, He revealed His plans for me.

"For I know the plans I have for you," declares the Lord, "plans to prosper you and not to harm you, plans to give you hope and a future." **(Jeremiah 29:11)**

And oh how grateful I am for this future, for this life I have been given.

My Journey with God on the Road to Recovery

By: Katie LaBlanc

My story is a little bit different, in the sense that I wasn't traveling far from home when I felt God's presence in my life. I was however, stopped on the road when I knew that God was reaching out to me. I didn't realize it was God at the time, but as my journey to recovery began, it became clear to me that this was in fact God's work.

In September of 2010, I was arrested for my third OWI. At this point in my life, I was in the darkest of places. Throughout the years that I was drinking, my relationship with my family was rocky, and at times, non-existent due to my own choosing. I burned bridges with what were once best friends, and I constantly carried around an "I don't care about anything" kind of attitude. I went from job to job, was drinking heavily on a daily basis, and I had no regard for my life, let alone anyone else's. So, when I was arrested, well, it was just another sucky thing that was happening to me. Looking back now, this "sucky" thing was the best thing that happened to me.

I remember calling my mom and dad from jail to tell them what happened and where I was; and to be honest, because I needed my parents help once again. As I was talking to my dad, the words "I drink every day and I need help" came out of my mouth. Being honest was far from the kind of person I was, so I was shocked that I even said that. Come to find out, being honest about my alcoholism was not me speaking, but God, and the beginning of my life changing process.

I began attending AA meetings on a daily basis, got a sponsor, and started working the steps of the program. My desire to drink was lifted immediately. As I would share my story and everything that happened over my 12 year drinking career, I very distinctly remember people telling me over and over again that my third OWI was a "blessing in disguise." At first, I didn't quite see it as such because of all the consequences I was facing. However, I was sober, I had the support of my family and friends, and I was slowly learning that this was part of God's plan for me.

Throughout my sobriety, my relationship with God became stronger and stronger. I knew and believed that I had to go through everything I did in my life in order to have the life God chose for me. As I continued to go to AA meetings, I was learning who I was without alcohol, and I liked me. I was continuously rebuilding my relationships with my family and friends, who happened to be there for me through it all. I stayed sober no matter what and I was becoming the person God intended me to be. I could now truly be thankful for hitting rock bottom because this was God's way of showing me a life I never thought imaginable. Don't get me wrong, it took a lot of work; but this time I knew I had God with me every step of the way. Sure, I faced trials and tribulations and I had my ups and downs, but it wasn't anything that God and I couldn't handle together.

When the time came to face my consequences for my OWI, I was sentenced a total of 6 months with work release. Of course that was a devastating blow. I was scared and nervous; but with God's help I was ready to face my consequences. It was a tough time because for so long I had this routine of attending AA meetings daily and going to mass 2-3 times a week. I was worried that I might be too distant from the things that made my life purposeful. But as I was told many times, "If you find yourself distant from God, ask yourself who moved," and so with that, I was determined to always make my relationship with God a priority, no matter how hard it got.

I had made it through my sentencing and was right back at my AA meetings and attending church. I continued to work the steps of the program with my sponsor and my relationships with my family and friends became better than they had ever been. God continued to reveal more and more to me throughout my sobriety and I never stopped being thankful to have Him in my life.

As I sit here today, February 20, 2017, I have been sober for almost 6.5 years: 2,144 days to be exact. Not a day goes by where I don't ask God for the strength to stay sober and I thank Him every night for my sobriety for that day. I would not have the life I have today if it wasn't for God. He saved me. He's blessed me with an incredible sober life, and getting a third OWI was most definitely a blessing in disguise.

I hope my story inspires you to know God and to believe that there is always hope. I will leave you with a song that makes me feel close to God, and reminds me of what He did and continues to do for me.

The Summons

"Will you come and follow me if I but call your name?

Will you go where you don't know and never be the same?

Will you let my love be shown? Will you let my name be known?

Will you let my life be grown in you and you in me?

Will you leave yourself behind if I but call your name?

Will you care for cruel and kind and never be the same?

Will you risk the hostile stare should your life attract or scare?

Will you let me answer prayer in you and you in me?

Will you let the blinded see if I but call your name?

Will you set the prisoners free and never be the same?

Will you kiss the leper clean and do such as this unseen, and admit to what I mean in you and you in me?

Will you love the "you" you hide if I but call your name? Will you quell the fear inside and never be the same?

Will you use the faith you've found to reshape the world around, through my sight and touch and sound in you and you in me?

Lord your summons echoes true when You but call my name. Let me turn and follow you and never be the same.

In your company I'll go where Your love and footsteps show. Thus I'll move and live and grow in you and you in me."

God is Alive and Well in Kathmandu, Nepal

By: Doreen Robak

I had never traveled out of the country. However, I always wanted to. This was the perfect opportunity for me. My daughter Shannon was an experienced world traveler and had been to Nepal twice. The people in Nepal stole her heart and she was drawn back. For good reason.

The majority of the people in Nepal are poor. Very poor. If I hadn't seen it with my own eyes, I wouldn't have believed how many of them live in conditions like they do. It's not unusual for a family of five to live in a single room. They sleep, cook, and eat in that one room. Electricity goes on and off throughout the day. So, when it's on, you better do your cooking and boil your water to drink.

Cold water bucket showers will wake you up in the morning. Of course, you don't waste water. You take your bucket shower, rinse the soap off of your body that goes into another bucket, and then use that water to flush down the toilet. Well, not actually flush. Pour down the toilet. That would be if you're lucky enough to have a toilet.

Many people use squat toilets which I was lucky enough to escape from using. I calculated how much I was drinking and where we were going, in order to avoid using a squat toilet. My calculations paid off! And...I'm not ashamed to admit that! Shannon thought I should at least experience a squat toilet once. I thought about it for a second, and thought maybe I should since I was in Kathmandu and I should do as the Nepali people do. However, after enough thought, I couldn't convince myself that would be a good experience to talk about, so I monitored everything that went into my stomach. No squat toilet experience for me! We are surely blessed in the United States of America. Our toilets are a beautiful thing. Life is good.

GOD is good. All the time.

If you visit Nepal and do not sense God's presence, there is something very wrong. His presence is so strong, not only in Nepal but everywhere. He just makes himself a bit more noticeable in Nepal. There is something about the people of Nepal that really stood out for me. Although they are poor, and have very little material things, they have a peace about them that I wish I could have bottled up and brought home with me to share with others.

God is first in the lives of the people in Nepal. Colorful prayer flags drape from building to building. Small Buddhist temples, located on the streets, are open to the public where people pray openly. Prayer wheels are found in the temples and along the streets where you see people walking and spinning the wheels while they pray.

Small business owners have bowls of incense burning at the doorstep of their shop announcing that prayers have been made in hopes of a successful day. When I say "shops", it's not a store as you would see in America. The best way to describe their shops would be a small space that they sell their goods in. Many people sell fruit and meat on the streets and I didn't see many things that were refrigerated. Including the meat. Needless to say, I didn't eat any meat while I was there. That is part of the life in Kathmandu and the streets are crowded with people.

GOD is good. All the time.

I sensed God's presence in the children of the school where Shannon taught. There was a young man with Muscular Dystrophy, in a wheelchair. If you saw the streets of Kathmandu, you would know immediately that getting around in a wheelchair was far from easy.

Many of the roads are dirt and filled with cars, motorcycles, people, and not to mention the sacred cows, chickens, and wild dogs. Oh yes. God has all of His creatures living together in Kathmandu. I'm pretty convinced the cows own Kathmandu. They stop traffic. Don't even think about doing anything to harm them. They are sacred!

There are no traffic lights or lanes that are marked. We used the local transportation of course because that's how Shannon travels. We were literally crammed into buses. Or should I say tin boxes with three wheels that thought it was a bus! It's hot, there's no air conditioning, and the windows are open so dust from the road comes in.

Getting back to the young man in the wheelchair. What caught my attention was how his friends took care of him. He was included in everything. We visited his home and his friends were there playing a game with him. On that day, there was something I felt very strongly. God's love was pouring out onto that young man. God had given that young man strength through his friends. Being handicapped and living in poor conditions, are simply, not easy. Yet, that young man was happy and so pleased we visited him.

GOD is good. All the time.

As I traveled in Nepal, I wore my cross necklace. That caught the eyes of two young girls. One of the girls came up to me and asked, "So, Jesus is your

God?" I smiled and told her yes. I told her that there is one God that cares for everyone in the whole world, as that is what I believe. She smiled and while walking away, replied, "Yes. There is one God."

The other little girl simply asked me if I was a Christian. Of course, I told her I was. She just smiled. I have a feeling she wasn't sure what a "Christian" did or how one may act! When was the last time someone asked you about your religion? Maybe if we asked more questions to each other about beliefs, we would have a better understanding of each other. I sure learned a lot about people who praise Buddha. I have a feeling Buddha and Jesus may be very good friends!

GOD is good. All the time!

On one of the first mornings we arrived in Nepal, we traveled via bus to the school. We traveled on the bus as far as we were able and then walked about 20 minutes the rest of the way to school. There was a bakery on the way. Anyone that knows me, knows I have to find the best bakery in each town I travel to.

Shannon was familiar with one certain bakery, but it wasn't the bakery that was special. It's what Shannon did when we got there. Both Shannon and I stayed away from meat while visiting in Nepal. In fact, my diet consisted of rice, shortbread cookies from the bakery, and crackers. I didn't want to get sick and need to use a squat toilet. My plan worked. Anyways, on that morning, Shannon ordered a bottle of water, which was warm due to no refrigeration, and a pizza bread with meat and cheese on it. I was surprised she ordered that as there was no way I was ever going to taste that meat! Shannon had her purchase bagged up and as we walked out, I asked her about it. She said she knew of a lady she was going to give it to.

We proceeded to walk down the street and Shannon approached a home-less, elderly woman, bent down, and gave her the water and food. I hadn't seen the woman sitting there when we approached the bakery and asked Shannon when she saw her. Shannon said she knew her from previous visits to Nepal and had given her food in the past. She was hoping she would still be there. Sure enough! That made our day and obviously that woman's day! By the time we left Nepal, that homeless woman had a new umbrella, a new blanket, and a fuller stomach!

GOD is good. All the time!

When we visited Nepal, the owners of the school that Shannon volunteered at, were gracious enough to allow us to actually stay in their home, while they stayed at the school! If that isn't God's love shining down and being shared with us, I don't know what is.

Families of the children invited us over for meals and shared their food with us. The little food they had. They shared smiles and kindness, as they had plenty of that to offer. People helped us with directions, and were simply kind, as it was pretty obvious that we stood out in the crowd.

A very important place that we visited was Pashupatinath-the cremation site of those that have died. In Nepal, when a loved one dies, their body is burned along the banks of the Bagmati River. The ashes are then put directly into the river. This place is open to everyone, including the public and tourists who can come to watch.

To be honest, I felt this was disrespectful to the families as tourists were able to view the burning of the body as families were grieving. Some tourists were talking with their guides as this was going on. I'm not sure why they needed an explanation from a guide to tell them what was happening, as it was pretty clear.

Shannon and I didn't stay long at this site. I felt God strongly surrounding the deceased person and their families. While observing this ceremony, God had a strong message for everyone that was observing. Life is about love. Plain and simple.

All of God's people, no matter where they are in the world, have loved ones. They celebrate with them, laugh with them, cry with them, and when a family member returns home to God, all of their loved ones grieve and mourn their loss. It doesn't matter what language anyone speaks or where they come from. God is all about love. He is with all of us and makes this very clear. All of us need to pay very close attention to His message.

God is good. All the time!

God is obviously present everywhere I've traveled in the United States. I tell people to travel with me because all always goes well. I have God and His angels with me all of the time. If you look for God's presence, it will literally smack you in the face. It just takes a few more slaps for some than it does for others!!

All of the people around the world have many things in common. People want peace, love, food, shelter, and to simply be safe. If each of us would do one nice thing each day for another person, it would make a world of difference. Not to mention how good it will make you feel.

I traveled to Nepal following the terrible earthquake that hit those beautiful people in 2015. They pulled together rebuilding their homes and temples.

Some of the buildings are standing with bamboo poles for support. The people of Nepal drew upon their faith in God to rebuild. They remain strong, peaceful, beautiful people. God is with them. God is with all of us. You don't need to look far to see and feel His love and presence. It's right in front of you.

God is inside each of us. Let His presence be known, no matter where you live or travel to.

GOD is good! All the time! And, all the time, God is good!

Plans for Me

By: Wanda Lucas

"For I know the plans I have for you," declares the Lord, "plans to prosper you and not to harm you, plans to give you hope and a future."
– Jeremiah 29:11

"Your luggage was not on your flight from Miami. I'm sorry", the Latam airline representative politely explained to me.

"So what do I need to do to receive my luggage?" I said in a clearly agitated voice. "You know, I asked American Airlines if I needed to claim my bag in Miami and check it with your airline directly and they told me no." I tried extremely hard not to show my irritation but I felt all of this could have been avoided. "What a way to start this trip," I said under my breath. "I came here hoping to make a difference in the lives of individuals living in Peru along with other people affected by cancer. Don't they know cancer is awful?" I mumbled to myself.

Once I gave them my contact information, the address of where I would be staying in Lima, and the phone number of the coordinator, I felt a little better. I took a deep breath and proceeded to the airport exit to look for the driver who, I was told, would be holding a sign that read, "Cross Cultural Solutions". He better be there, I thought. I do not need any more aggravation.

Walking towards the airport exit, I noticed that individuals in the airport were wearing a great deal of cologne. I listened to conversations in Spanish and smiled. I thought to myself, "Those Spanish lessons are paying off, because I can understand a good amount of what is being said."

My body relaxed once I found the driver. I walked up to him, smiled, and proudly said, "Hola, me llamo Wanda Lucas, senor!"

He gave me a big smile in return and said, "Ah, si! Senora Lucas, mucho gusto. We are waiting for two more people."

I decided to wait by the window so I could people watch as we waited for the rest of my group. I knew their names but wondered if we would be guarded with each other. After all, this was a trip where we would have to be vulnerable with a group of strangers. I knew I was in for a huge personal challenge because I have always lived my life so privately. So, I waited, watched, and wondered. The airport was very busy and it was only 7:00 a.m.

People moved about quickly and with a purpose. They greeted, hugged and kissed each other on the cheek displaying warmth and compassion.

The others arrived shortly. We exchanged pleasantries and took a moment to size each other up. In my mind, the three of us knew that this trip was going to be different and it was beginning at this very moment. We followed our driver to the van that would take us to our residence for the next two weeks. Once we reached the van, I was startled by its appearance. I was truly not expecting a Lincoln town car, but this vehicle was definitely showing its age and use. The interior was clean, although the seats were rather worn. We hopped in and quickly engaged in a conversation. We shared our type of cancer and the length of time since diagnosis - typical and predictable topics when cancer survivors meet for the first time.

As the conversation continued we made remarks every now and then about the bumpy ride and how the van's engine was anything but quiet. We shared a few chuckles, which aided in loosening the mood and making us feel better after overnight flights.

From time to time, I would gaze out of the window, observing the hustle and bustle of the people on this random Saturday morning. The movement, the traffic, and noise helped me tap into the life of the people. There were lots of retail and industrial places on the busy and littered roadway giving me a sense of comfort since it was similar to other places I had visited.

We soon arrived in the Lima district of Barranco, our new home. The information we had received was accurate - the accommodations in the former Catholic convent were basic but clean. We were greeted by the first person in our group to arrive outside of the facilitators. As the four of us sat by the pool and got to know each other, we coined ourselves the "Core Four".

As the day went on, we greeted each newly arriving group member and also took the time to walk around our new neighborhood. We quickly found the always important Starbucks, cute stores and restaurants, and noticed the town was home to lots of wonderful murals. I loved the bridges, activity, colors, cobblestone streets, and the people. Comfort in this new place came quickly.

"The compound" as I called it, with its basic appearance truly provided the right ingredients for nurturing the development of a tribe. The dining room held community tables, the living room had large comfortable sofas, and the expansive grounds provided places for group activities that were especially powerful when held under the stars.

The grounds overlooked the Pacific Ocean; allowing us to experience breathtaking sunsets which calmed our souls; stressed by the realities of living with a disease.

That first night, as my two roommates slept, I thought about the newness of my current situation. I was here with the organization, A Fresh Chapter (AFC),that provides opportunities for individuals who have been affected by cancer to start fresh and find a new purpose in their lives. My initial interest was due to the international volunteering experience. Since it had been more than a decade since my last missionary trip, I felt it was time to serve once again.

I laughed as I thought about my initial phone interview with the founder of A Fresh Chapter. I cried the entire time as she asked questions, which required me to pull out feelings that I had long buried relative to my cancer diagnosis. Then, I remembered the emotions I had because of those feelings and the power they had over my life. It had taken a while to fully profess those feelings; yet the freedom I was experiencing was nothing short of miraculous.

I gave myself permission to admit and share with my community that I was in fact broken, because I was harboring pain I had never released. Remarkably, my community of friends and associates back home responded with support that literally knocked me off of my feet. My journey had begun.

The idea of impacting someone's life in a short amount of time was intriguing; yet I was about to learn that was not God's sole plan for me during this trip. Each morning we were taken to a Catholic run housing facility not far from our compound. My volunteer assignment, with two other participants, was working with young girls who had been rescued from human trafficking situations. Although a language barrier existed, it did not interfere with our ability to connect with them. The situation compelled us to bond on a different level - one more spiritual and with fewer expectations.

The blessing was that these connections were beyond what I could have ever imagined. God showed me what could take place when the intention is pure and unassuming. He spoke volumes to me through the precious girls I worked with every day.

"Buenos dias!" the girls would say every morning when we walked into the room. Their smiles and excitement in seeing us warmed my heart daily.

"Buenos dias chicas! Como esta?" They would greet each of us with hugs and kisses on the cheek.

Their custom became our custom. Their smiles were infectious and I often wondered what they secretly thought about strangers coming to spend time with them every day.

These girls, wounded and broken in unimaginable ways, found strength in their situations and were able to exhibit a willingness to connect. They showed us so much about the resilience of the human spirit. Each day, I would take a few moments to step back and just observe them as they worked on that day's tasks. These private moments of watching them allowed me to see the hurt in their eyes. My heart ached deeply as I noticed their smiles disappear and their eyes become less bright when they were not actively engaged with us.

I could see their pain on them because their faces seemed to be absent of life and light. I often choked back tears, trying not to imagine the hurt they had experienced in their short lives. I became angry thinking about the horrible people who were responsible for their pain. It was clear that each girl, with her individual personality and equally horrific story, simply wanted appropriate attention, compassion, and acceptance.

"How do they keep going each day?" I asked myself, "How can they trust us not to harm nor mislead them?" I wondered and they showed me. They simply showed up, each and every day. Their behavior assured me that they believed in better days. They took risks by extending trust and ultimately demonstrated a spirit I had not expected. My girls showed me how you can move forward when you have faith.

My special girl, who I will call Eve, was a dark-haired fifteen-year old who wore glasses. There was just something about her – something familiar. On the very first day, she seemed to catch my glance and look at me as if she already knew me. I noticed her passion for school and desire for perfection got tickled because she would always sit next to me at the table. When we started an activity of painting one day, I watched as Eve took her time to think about what she wanted to create. She didn't rush when she started and quietly shared more about herself with me. With every stroke of her brush, she carefully laid out her story on the paper.

I learned that she was from the mountains of Peru. She spoke many words leading me to believe she missed being there with her animals. "Mi hermanos" and "mi padre," she whispered as she drew human figures. It was clear that she missed the family she may never see again. It was quite noticeable that she never mentioned her mother. I later learned that some of the girl's mothers were the very ones who put them into the trafficking situation. My Eve became my special girl, my daughter, "mi hija".

I noticed many things about my girl. She would cover her mouth whenever she laughed as if she was afraid to let loose. She always wore long sleeves and pants. She was always the one willing to help the youngest girl learn new things. I suggested, as best I could in Spanish, that she should become a teacher. She let me know that she wanted to be a veterinarian instead.

I wondered if she would be allowed to attend college, especially after seeing her work so hard with her studies. Based on seeing the other girl's homework assignments, Eve seemed to be ahead of them in school. I chuckled when I realized I couldn't help her with certain subjects. "Too advanced for me," I thought to myself. Eve and I spent a great deal of time in our own little world trying our best to learn the other's language.

On one particular day, Eve grabbed a book and put it out in front of me. She wanted me to read to her – in Spanish. I reacted to her instructions feeling my body soften and noticing my hands naturally come to rest in my lap. Eve wanted me to learn her language. As I read the story of Hansel and Gretel, I found myself smiling because the story was never sweeter.

"Brujah!" I said excitedly as I read about the witch and we both laughed.

I loved when Eve took the time to correct me when I didn't enunciate a word correctly. She encouraged me to say the word over and over until I said it properly. When I read the words well, she celebrated and gave me the thumbs up (as I apparently do, a great deal.) My sweet girl was my teacher-exhibiting confidence and comfort with me. Not just on that day but every day. I learned the beauty of relinquishing power, of letting go and letting God direct you. I felt that she was simply glad that I was there and that I saw her, acknowledged and appreciated her for whom she was. In response, my wonderful Eve taught me gratefulness.

I think about Eve a lot and writing about her has helped me discover what I found so special about her. In some ways, she reminded me of a younger version of myself. Like me, she was quiet, shy, and in some ways awkward. She was also smart, focused, and willing to help others. Looking back, I now know why it was so important for me to write a personal note to her before I left Peru. My note read:

"*Tu eres muy bonita y muy inteligente. (You are very pretty and very intelligent.) Estoy tan alegre de haberle conocido. (I am so glad that I met you.) Te veo a ti como una hija! (I look at you as my special daughter!) Quiero decirte que todas las cosas son posibles con Dios. (I want you to know that all things are possible with God).*"

Besitos, (kisses) Wanda

I wanted to impart special words of encouragement to her because I knew the power of words. I wanted to leave something with her, secretly hoping that she would never forget me.

One day we worked alongside them helping them with their kitchen duties. Their actions were simple, deliberate, and completed with a prideful demonstration. They worked as a team and gracefully invited us into their activity. The kitchen was basic and while I noticed what was missing I also learned that it did not matter in the completion of the tasks. I took it in and realized that happiness can come in those moments of simplicity - in the absence of gluttony.

As I think back over my time with the girls, there was nothing spectacular that we did with them. We simply offered our time. We went there to offer friendship and support and much to our surprise we were the ones who were greatly changed.

At times, these young girls took on adult roles and showed us how to get back up when you have been knocked down. Their presence proved that you can flourish even when your plan is disrupted. They were willing to show vulnerability because of their faith. I think about my girls every day and still wonder if they will ever be fully free.

It took me a while to process everything that happened to me on that trip. I found it challenging to describe it to people who didn't understand the experience of having a life changing illness. The bonds that were formed on that trip are indescribable, unique, and everlasting.

I learned many lessons in those 16 days that will stay with me forever. It isn't always about reaching a destination. The journey and what you learn and experience along the way is generally what is most beautiful. My trip to Peru reminded me, once again, to let go and let God. Thank you Lord.

Jesus Takes the Wheel

By: Courtney Mulica

Growing up in Michigan and going to college in Green Bay, Wisconsin, I am no stranger to back country roads and cold, harsh winters. I actually pride myself in my strong midwestern roots where I mucked horse stalls and drove through some of the worst blizzards at what now seems like a very young age. I find myself laughing a bit when all of Fort Collins shuts down as soon as the weather man announces that snow is "coming".

All that aside, nothing could prepare me for the car accident I experienced in the beginning of 2017. I know this book is about finding God through travel, but mine was not to a faraway place. My experience with God happened while traveling very close to home. It was Tuesday morning and like every other day during my work week, my alarm went off at 4:35am. I jumped out of bed, into my workout clothes, stumbled through brushing my teeth, and was out the door at 4:55am. My friend who I carpool with jumped in my car and off we went. We were headed to our 5:15am workout to get our butts kicked; but little did I know what was in store for me that day.

Before that fateful morning, I had gone through a series of difficult transitions; and working out played an important role in getting me through all of it. After somewhat of a rough shift from full-time career woman to full-time stay-at-home mommy, I found myself a bit lost. Initially, it seemed like a no brainer to quit my job. When I dropped my baby off at daycare, I felt like my baby cub was being ripped away from his momma. I was overwhelmed with guilt: feeling like someone else was raising my child, that I wasn't pumping enough milk,that I was missing milestones, and due to complete exhaustion at the end of the day- from counting down the hours until he went to sleep, only so I could quickly inhale food and crash on the couch. I was not present in any facet of my life.

When I decided to take the plunge to stay home full-time, the first few months were great. I spent my days playing with Asher, going to the pool, going for walks, making him healthy snacks, and actually had time to have conversations over dinner with my husband. Life was good - I was on what felt like full-time vacation, I didn't have to answer to anyone, and I finally had time to tackle some of those house projects that I could never find the time to take care of.

Until one day, in what seemed like out of the blue, I woke up and realized all my friends were at work, I hadn't used my brain for anything besides baby talk, and hadn't changed out of my yoga pants or put on makeup since I decided to leave my career three months prior. I had all of the time in the world, yet I was too busy changing diapers, making snacks, and cleaning up to find the time to really exercise – or do anything by myself for that matter. I couldn't go to yoga because who would watch Asher? And I started to cringe at the idea of taking another walk around the same block that I had walked around every day for the last 90 days. It is easy to say that being a mom is enough, but when I stripped away my role as Assistant Marketing Director, it was hard to understand who I really was or what purpose I served.

I'm hardly the Martha Stewart type, so while thoughts of being a dreamy stay-at-home mom occurred to me, folding laundry and making dinner got old real fast. I was in the midst of an identity crisis and feeling a little depressed. I started to feel resentful for having worked so hard only to give up my career, and my independence, which I realized was a big part of who I am.

I knew I needed to make a change, and thought that a more regular exercise routine would at the very least get my endorphins going again. I decided to make the commitment to get up early before my husband went to work to get a workout in. I found that most of the time when I returned, Asher was still sleeping and I had enough time to jump in the shower and start my day. It was a game changer. Exercise made me happier, I had a better outlook on the start of the day, and I felt as if I finally belonged somewhere again. It was the first step that I took in order to find myself again, and it worked.

Now back to the seemingly normal morning of the accident. Colorado has always been known for extreme temperature variations with the winter of 2017 being no exception. We were in a pattern of record breaking warm days, followed by a drop in temperature, snow, and then back to 70 degrees – all in the course of a week.

On this particular morning there was a slight dusting of snow on the ground, but the roads seemed perfectly clear. We drove our usual way, leaving our neighborhood to turn onto a back country road where we chatted away about how tired we were and how crazy it was that we worked out this early. As we approached a stop sign I tried to slow down and realized that as I hit the brakes, I was sliding full speed towards the intersection. I had hit black ice and it felt as though we were skating across an ice rink.

On most mornings we were the only car on the road, and the worst that could have happened was that we would have slid into an open field. However, this morning was different. As we slid uncontrollably towards the intersection, I looked to my right and saw what I thought to be a semi-truck barreling down the road. I remember the very vivid thought that if we kept sliding towards the truck, we were not going to come out of it alive. Is this really how I am going to go out, on a random Tuesday morning?

To this day, I still can't wrap my head around the fact that in that moment, my gut reaction was to accelerate in an attempt to get out of the truck's way. I was gunning it towards a huge truck not knowing if we would hit head-on, he would T-bone us, or we would beat him.

Somehow we picked up speed, and plowed through the intersection. I screamed and for a brief second, thought that we made it through, when all of a sudden I heard the boom of the truck crashing into us. The impact jolted us sideways, sending my coffee cup flying and then instantly, the car came to a stop. Sitting there disoriented and drenched in coffee, my first thought was to make sure my friend was ok. Even as we reassured each other that we were in one piece, I was worried I was in a deep state of shock almost expecting something worse – checking myself over for blood or any sign of injury. Where was the other driver?

In an attempt to understand what had happened, we got out of the car to take a look at the remains of my Acadia. At that moment, I knew it was a miracle that we were standing there. The truck hit us near the tail end of the passenger side, and basically drove through the entire back end of my car. There was not much left to the back of the car but we were relatively un- touched. What the he** just happened? The other driver came over to see if we were ok, he had spun three times and ended up in a ditch down the road. He was driving an F350 truck (not a semi but a very large truck) and said he was going at least 50 mph. When he saw us sliding, he attempted to slow down but realized he had hit the same patch of black ice. He said the roads were completely dry up until that point.

Together we stood shaking from fear and the cold while we waited for the police to arrive. My friend's husband arrived at the scene and I remember being horrified as he drove up at the thought that I was the one to put his wife in such danger. He suggested I gather my things from my car for it was obvious it would be totaled.

Still a little disoriented, I began to collect anything I saw. The front of the ve- hicle was in perfect condition. When I tried to get into the back, the "what- ifs" started pouring through my mind. Because of the damage, I couldn't get through the back passenger door and had to climb through crumbles of glass to rip out the car seat that was secured in my back seat. What if Asher, my 18-month- old son had been in the car? What if the chance I took caused something horrific to happen to my friend? Why would I have accelerated if I was already out of control? What if I never had a chance to say goodbye to the people I love? A whirlwind of thoughts raced through my head.

I'll never forget being dropped off at my house only to unload a couple of belongings: a single bluegrass cd, my registration, and my son's car seat and stroller. I think I was still in shock while explaining the situation to my husband. My friend and her husband showed such compassion, and reiterated over and over that we were so lucky because of my intuition.

I couldn't shake the thought of why I accelerated in the first place, and felt guilty for putting ourselves in that situation. Although I tend to think I can be pretty intuitive, I couldn't take the credit for this miracle. I knew it wasn't me that made that decision; that it was a power much greater and extraordinary. And for some reason, this feeling really shook me. It was the closest I have ever felt to God.

After making some phone calls to my insurance contacts and squeezing my little baby tight, I picked up the phone to call my parents. I seemed to hold it together until, while talking to my dad, I reached the point in the story where I explained that I had no idea how or why I was able to beat the truck, and how close it came to seriously hurting my friend and myself. With this realization, the tears and emotion came flooding out of me. It scared me that I didn't even understand why I took the chance that I had, and if that was the right judgement call.

On one hand it's safe to say it was the right call because we were alive. However, it was an inexplicable feeling to not understand where that would come from. When I spoke to my mom, I told her it was as if an angel took over. As she looked at the images of the demolished car, she said the song with the lyrics "Jesus took the wheel" kept coming to the forefront of her mind. As I replayed what happened over and over, I began to realize just how much of a miracle it was. There is no logical reasoning to explain how we survived, it could not be more clear that God was watching over us and quite literally pulling us out of harm's way.

The next few days were a bit of a roller coaster. Not only did I feel a little beat up physically, but emotionally I was fragile. Each morning I woke up I was completely grateful for another day. Temper tantrums from my little guy seemed cute and natural as opposed to frustrating. Normally with my "get it done" attitude, I would have been annoyed if the insurance company didn't return my calls promptly regarding the status of my vehicle; yet somehow I now had compassion and trust that they were working hard on their end. And frankly, I wasn't in a hurry to go anywhere.

In the moment, I couldn't quite understand why my husband didn't immediately have the same change in perspective that I had. Don't get me wrong, he was happy I was okay, but seemed to go about life like nothing had happened. Looking back, I think it's hard for anyone hearing the story to understand just how much of an act of God it was unless he/she experienced the miracle that I had.

Taking risks is part of my makeup, and I have made some reckless decisions where I have put myself in danger. But never did I expect that my life could be taken from me after a simple routine drive that I do every day.

A near-death experience would likely change anyone's outlook on life; and unfortunately when people are taken from us unexpectedly, it is usually a time where we all vow to not get caught up in the little things.

This experience of course put things into perspective; but what is even more powerful was the realization that although I have always *believed* it, I now *know* with 100% certainty that my path has been decided for me and God is always present along the way. Not just present on the special days, but on the random Tuesdays and every second in between.

Although I would never want to relive this experience, it was a wakeup call that I needed. In addition to my identity crisis, the year prior had not been an easy one: health issues affecting family, stress with my husband's job, feelings of loneliness, isolation, and sadness all had certainly tested my faith. It's almost as if God threw a bucket of cold water over my head and said "Wake up, I'm still here! I've got you!"

I wish I could say that every head flailing, biting, toddler meltdown since then has been handled with a smile, but I can't. It's still easy to get caught up in the little challenges of day-to-day life. However, my overall sense of trust in Him and my path has been profound, allowing me to feel more grounded and live more graciously, enjoying time with the people I love, and all of God's great gifts. And, although I'm still in transition, things have been on the up and up.

Opportunities have fallen into my lap and I'm now able to enjoy working part-time which gives me some independence, as well as the flexibility to spend time with my child. It seems as though the more trusting I am that everything will work out the way it's supposed to, things are falling into place more and more. I know the journey won't be perfect, but I know I'm in good hands and that feels pretty good.

"I believe in God not because my parents told me, not because my church told me, but because I experienced His goodness and mercy myself."

Butterfly by My Side

By: Devon Liebl

Sundays are a day to relax, refuel, and regenerate before another hectic week. I look forward to Sundays. It is the one day of the week that I get lost in my thoughts. I let my mind wander. I wake up, walk to my kitchen, make coffee and start meal planning. My Sundays are spent cooking. This habit of mine has become one of my therapies. My mind gets lost as I stand chopping the onion, browning the meat, and stirring the soup. I think about my week, my mistakes in the past, how thankful I am for the present. But most of the time, while I'm standing in my kitchen, my attention is on a certain picture on my cutting board. The photo is of my older sister, little sister, little brother and I. We are standing in our swimsuits posing on a beach in Marco Island, Florida.

February 24, 2012 started like most Saturday mornings. I woke up and enjoyed breakfast and a cup of coffee. This particular Saturday had a different feeling for a winter day in Chicago. The weather was in the upper 50's and the sun was shining bright. A day like this in the dead of winter meant getting outside. A few friends and I hit the streets of Chicago, which were filled with walkers, shoppers and diners. Everyone was trying to get a little piece of the warm sun. We took a long walk to grab lunch. The day was perfect. I felt high on life. This sunny, warm winter day felt too good to be true.

After lunch we made our way to a local bar for a few rounds of pool. As we played pool, my cell phone rang. "Dad" lit up on my screen. I let it go to voicemail. After hitting my shot I listened to his message. In a warm but somewhat dreadful tone, he asked for me to call him back immediately. My stomach began to tighten, my heart was racing, and my palms were sweating. I always trust my first gut instinct. Something wasn't right. I got my coat on and headed home to make the call to my Dad. Just like that I received the worst news of my life. My big sister Ashley had passed away suddenly, the night before. I stood motionless. Time had stopped.

Immediately I panicked. I never said sorry; I never made amends; I will never be able to look her in the eyes and tell her how much I love her. My life had changed.

The next thing I knew, I was standing in front of a crowded church, reading my big sister's eulogy. Numbness, sadness, confusion, regret, anger, all rushed through my mind and body. I stood there, behind the microphone, next to the altar, in a place I felt comfortable and familiar with-my grade school church. I looked down at Ashley's casket, and it hit me that I would never physically see my sister's face again. My eyes closed, I fought back tears, whispered to my big sister "please stay with me, give me the strength to make this perfect for you."

With my head down, I stared at my piece of paper. As I started speaking about my big sister, her face flashed in my mind. I was remembering her perfect smile, infectious laugh, compassion for others, and the love she carried in her heart. She had an incredible outlook on life. Growing up she would encourage me to, "Never wish your life away." She inspired me to follow my heart, follow my dreams, and stay strong. I needed this advice more than anything at that moment.

After my sister's passing, I was angry, regretful, and in denial. Years before my sister passed away we had an unfortunate falling out. It started out as a sibling fight, but as time went on our stubbornness grew towards one another. I wanted an apology. She, on the other hand didn't think what she did was wrong. My immaturity and stubbornness brought lost time to our relationship. The only thing I could do, was get angry at my stupidity. I started praying every night. Each night I would close my eyes, I pictured Ashley sitting, to the right side of God.

I would first ask Him "Please God, watch over my sister. Please bring her happiness, love and peace." Then I would ask my big sister for forgiveness. "Ash, I am so sorry I wasn't there for you. I'm sorry I gave up on you. Please forgive me. And know how much I miss you and how much I love you. Goodnight. See you in the morning." Every night I repeated the same prayer. Each morning I woke up, hoping for a sign or something to answer my question, "why?" Why did this have to happen to my sister and why wasn't I able to see her one last time?

Over the next few years, I would oftentimes sit on my couch and pull out a box that held my sister's belongings: CDs she made for me, and cards she had given me. One night I pulled out the box and put on the song, "Hear You Me", by Jimmy Eat World on repeat. The lyrics, "What would you think of me now? So lucky, so strong, so proud?" This was repeating in my ears as I started pulling out cards and pictures. I took out a card she had given to me right before I moved away to college. I opened it and tears started rolling down my face as I looked at her handwriting and read, "Tough times don't last but tough people do." And then it hit me. I got an urgency to take a trip, to travel, to explore. God, in His mysterious way, showed me a sign that night. He put an idea in my mind that He would show me how to live life differently, starting at that moment. My big sister would live vicariously through me.

My sister was a young thirty-two years old when she passed away. My own thirty-second birthday was approaching and I was scared. I felt so young and had so much life ahead of me. How could I be turning the same age as my big sister when her life ended?

I made a decision. Something inside of me evolved, a sense of eagerness hit me. I would travel; get away. My sister and I would take an adventure; explore the world on her birthdays, on the anniversary of her death, and for other special occasions. I'd make the hard times better times. Instead of reliving a bad memory, I would make new meaningful memories. Ashley may not be physically present, but she is present every day in my heart. Her and I would take this adventure together. God was answering my prayers. He was giving me signs.

For my thirty-second birthday, I wanted to get away. This new outlook on adventure and traveling took me to Vancouver, Canada. I sat on the plane, staring out at the clouds, listening to the O.A.R. song *Gift*. The lyrics in my headphones "I can see you now, it's like you're never gone. From dusk til dawn, you soldiered on. Like each day was a gift" brought a sudden sadness. The sadness was because I realized my sister would never experience the beauty of our world that I had set off to explore. Following the sadness however, a sensation of peace and numbness filled my body.

I finally felt close to my sister up in the clouds. I looked out of the window and deep into the clouds. This image of my sister sitting to the right side of God crossed my mind. It was the same image I saw every night when I would pray. This feeling of comfort, as I started having a conversation with my sister, brought tears to my eyes. On that airplane, I finally felt my sister and I making amends. I could hear her voice, "Dee, it's going to be ok. I need you to make the most of your life, kiddo. Treat every day as a gift. Give love to those who surround you. Keep making me proud. I'm always with you. Keep looking for the signs." I was ready to show my big sister this world through my eyes, through my love and my passion for life.

I've approached traveling differently since the moment on that airplane. For each destination I visit, I now take a moment, look to my left, and imagine my sister standing right beside me. Her hair up in a bun pulled away from her face, her wide bright smile, and her dimples shining.

I've stood on Kitsilano Beach in Vancouver with the sun shining bright on my face, listening to water splash as it hit the surface, looking out and beyond to the mountain tops. I could feel God's and my sister's presence. Calmness, relaxation, and happiness came over me. I whispered to them "Thank you for giving me this new perspective on beauty."

I've made a trip back to Disney World to the same place my family and I would vacation to growing up. My family and I made many memories during our trips to Disney. One ride Ashley and I would go on a countless number of times was Big Thunder Mountain. As soon as we would get off the ride we would sprint right back into line. As I stood in line for Big Thunder Mountain as an adult, memories of her and I standing together as little girls came back to me, ready to take on this runaway railroad. There I was, looking to my left, whispering to Ashley "Should we go for the front or the back?" There I was, arms up, wind blowing in my face, screaming and laughing like we were kids again.

A summer trip to Red Rocks Park in the mountains of Colorado for a day of hiking, turned out to be the start of my forever with the love of my life. I was proposed to. As I climbed the terrain to a cliff, looking out at the stunning views, I whispered to my left "Thank you Ash, for giving me the strength to always follow my heart." Standing on that cliff, surrounded by God's creation, a wave of emotions came over me. My mind slowed down, calmness enveloped my body, and my heart filled with happiness. Stopping time to enjoy a moment, to feel God's presence.

My most recent adventure was to Cobh, Ireland: the Titanic's last port in 1912. A church, St. Colman's Cathedral sits overlooking the Cork Harbor. I stood outside this church, looking at the boats passing through. A butterfly flew in front of my face. I stood motionless as it slowly lowered itself to the ground. Butterflies have become a sign to me, letting me know that my sister is present. Each time I have an encounter, I give my sister a hello.

There was something special about this church. I walked in, and as soon as I entered, my eyes filled with tears. I was overcome with emotion. I took a seat in a pew and started praying. Tears rolled down my face as I connected with God. I sat in that pew, thanking Him over and over for His strength, His signs and the prayers He answered. In His miraculous ways, He opened my heart and made me realize what needed to be done in order to feel closer to my sister.

Over the past few years, on every trip I have taken, I've been able to connect with Ashley. I hear her voice, I see her smile, and I look for her signs. The anger and regret I felt for so many years after her passing began to slip away. My outlook on life had never felt so clear.

Every Sunday morning as I stand in my kitchen, looking at that picture, I hear her whisper "Dee, bring that smile today. Show love and happiness to those around you. Live today to its fullest. Keep making me proud. I'm right here." My big sister Ashley will forever be my butterfly: slowly flying by my side, showing me signs of her presence.

God Loves You

By: Tiffany Robak

I was trying to sleep, completely sunken into a pile of soft cushions that made a mattress, hoping and praying there was not a tarantula crawling in my sheets, or worse, lice on my pillow. I have a horrible fear of lice. It's weird, it started in childhood; the fact that these bugs can multiply exponentially and get on, and live on everything, really freaks me out. This fear resurfaced when I was sleeping at an orphanage in Honduras with my older sister.

It was rumored that some of the adorable little kids had lice. I tried to play it cool, but I knew my sister was freaking out a little bit too. My sister was a world traveler and volunteering in an orphanage for two months. I had just finished job training and had two weeks before I started work, so I decided to join her.

It was November 2013; I was 25 years old and I had been rejected from medical school earlier that year. I decided to look for other career options, and came across a position in medical sales, servicing orthopedic implants. Prior to finding this position, I had kept my blinders on, doing whatever I could to be accepted into medical school. I never thought about another career path besides medicine, and now that I was redirected, I found myself feeling and fearing a lack of fulfillment in my new position.

The year prior, I graduated with a Master's degree in the biomedical sciences. The year before that, I had volunteered in the AmeriCorps program, working with Latino patients in a community health center, providing health education on diabetes.

Most recently, I had been working as a clinical research assistant collecting sputum samples for an influenza study. In my attempt to be accepted to medical school, I had followed everyone's advice: I gained clinical experience, I volunteered, I worked in a lab, I took the MCAT three times to increase my score, I even obtained a graduate degree to boost my science GPA, and still, I did not even get one interview.

So instead of pursuing medicine and applying a second time, I decided to look around and explore other career options. I thought being rejected after putting forth that much effort must have been a sign. I needed to create an alternative option for myself. I ended up finding the job in medical sales; the medical aspect seemed to draw me in; was that a sign directing me *back* to medicine? I wasn't sure. I participated in a 3-month training program in Indiana for this company and became lucky enough to get a job at home, in Milwaukee. I asked for two weeks off before I started my permanent position so I could travel to Honduras, where thoughts changed and faith became my answer to everything.

Although I had decided not to apply to medical school that application cycle, I knew my MCAT score would be valid for applications one more year. Even though the pressure was off because I had the opportunity to pursue which-ever career I wanted, the pressure was on because of the MCAT expiration date. I only had a few months to decide if I would discover a path for myself outside of medicine and let the dream of becoming a physician die forever. Nobody wants to take the MCAT four times, or at the very least, I did not.

When I thought about medicine now, I wasn't even sure if I knew why I had been pursuing a career in medicine. Did I actually want to be a doctor? Was I even qualified to be a doctor? Or did I just feel the need to obtain a presti-gious title to be somebody? I thought I had done everything to build my re-sume and appear qualified for medical school, yet I was still rejected; it was difficult to comprehend. I had a lot to think about and a lot to pray about. I felt as if I had to redefine myself, because before this, I only ever pictured myself as a physician.

During this trip, while contemplating my life purpose, I was reading a book called *Tattoos on the Heart: The Power of Boundless Compassion* by Father Gregory Boyle. It was more inspiring than I anticipated. I knew service and working with others was a large part of my life but I had lost touch with it. There was a quote from Father Boyle that stayed with me for quite some time. It read: "Kinship— not serving the other, but being one with the other... There is a world of difference in that."

And it struck me. A lot. The entire book struck me. Father Boyle was work-ing with gang members in Los Angeles, CA. He was opening his heart and his arms to their lost souls, knowing the goodness that lay within them. He lived in their neighborhood, he ate with them, he worked with them. He was "being one with them." Father Boyle's compassion inspired me, but it also made me realize that acts like those are not sought after, they are results of one following their heart. If I were ever to perform true service for others, I needed to find my own heart, and I needed to become one with others as well as one with myself.

So there I was, in an orphanage in Honduras, volunteering, something I usually enjoyed, but this time I had no passion for it at all and no promising passion for my future career in sales. I really enjoyed service, I did, and I knew volunteering in that orphanage would allow me to become one with the people of Honduras. It would also help me when I was working with diverse populations in my future career, on whichever path I chose; but this trip in particular helped me to realize that although spending time with others can be fulfilling to some, it felt as though I was missing my potential to be with others in my own way.

I still needed to focus on finding my heart and my true passion, as Father Gregory Boyle demonstrated. I wanted my life's purpose to utilize a skill that I possessed, that defined me. I thought about my skill set and I realized I did not possess any skills to provide an impact in the lives of others.

Although this was difficult to come to terms with, and I experienced this trip with a heavy heart, it ended up inspiring me in a subtle and unexpected way. It did not however, reignite my passion for service. I did not feel ready to reach out and provide service to others; I did not have a skill. I know service will always be a part of my life, but at that time, it was not enough for me to simply "spend time" with the children. I wanted to do more for them and people in general. I prayed a lot and my faith began to grow much stronger. During this trip, I realized, it did not matter where I *wanted* to go, I was going to end up where God needed me.

I somehow realized while reading that book, that God still needed me to pursue medicine, to work to help others improve their quality of life through health by being one with them; by hearing them, seeing them, recognizing them as their own path to health, with me simply as their guide. This was my passion and I should not give up. I should follow my own heart on the path to medicine, rather than trying to fit the stereotypical mold of medical school applicants.

Service is more effective when it is one's passion, when you are utilizing the skills God gave you to help others, and you are truly being yourself. Although I say this now, it is a constant struggle to be true to myself and follow my heart, because sometimes it is not that obvious, and it can be very scary. So after many months of prayer to be on the path God needed me, without any signs but the gut feelings and constant thoughts about medical school, I decided off blind faith to pursue medicine again, but this time, in the way my heart was guiding me. So, I turned back to medicine with full force and full faith.

I began discovering how medicine would fit me rather than how I would fit medicine, as I had mistakenly done in my first attempt. I wanted to be one with it and one with my patients. Rather than continuously feeling as if it were something to which I had to prove myself, I wanted to allow myself to stay true to my heart. I would follow the more "holistic" route of Osteopathy, and when the time came, I would let God decide my specialty.

I matriculated into an Osteopathic medical school, where I could learn to physically and metaphorically touch people to help them heal themselves.

The spring of 2015, about four months before matriculation, I visited the medical university's campus for the first time. I flew out to Colorado to follow the path on which God had placed me, I drove to the school, and left crying. It was in the middle of nowhere, no restaurants, no gas stations, no food of any kind was within sight. It didn't even have a coffee shop or a cafeteria and the closest of these was a fifteen-minute drive away. I couldn't believe I was moving to Colorado by myself, no boyfriend, far from home, ready to embark on a stressful, isolating journey in an even more isolating university than I could have imagined. My mom gave me "the out." "If you don't want to do this, you don't have to," she said to me. But I had to, there was no other path I wanted to be on, no other way I could picture myself being "one with others," and ultimately, no other path I *needed* to be on. I was guided to this one.

On the way home from that trip, with a heavy heart, once again, I sat on the plane in silence. I closed my eyes but didn't sleep and just felt complete sadness; sadness about the school, about relationships in my life, or lack thereof, and about a close relative that was recently diagnosed with a chronic illness. Why was I not more excited about something I had worked so hard to achieve? Better yet, why was God sending me there to embark on this path alone? Besides a polite greeting, it wasn't until we were waiting to deplane that the woman next to me began to talk to me. Nothing of interest, just polite conversation until she finished with "God Bless You." Having not heard that in a while, my face may have lit up a little bit and I returned the blessing to her.

I walked off the plane and when I reached the airport, she came running after me. She looked slightly apprehensive but knew what she wanted to say, and that I would be open to hearing it. She said to me: "I'm getting a really strong message and I need to tell you that God heals the brokenhearted, and He wants you to know He loves you." Every piece of my body felt the truth of her words and tears streamed down my face. I wanted to talk to her more but she walked away and I never saw her again. To me, this was a sign I was on the right path, that God was guiding me to a career that was true to my heart, and also, to a love that would last forever, something in which I had been yearning for for quite some time.

Later that summer, I took the challenge of medical school with an open mind and an open heart. I engaged in a lot of extra-curricular activities, I dated a man with whom I fell in love for the first time, who supported my path and shared my faith, and I found school to be something I was good at, a place I was supposed to be. It seemed God had guided me to the perfect place.

I had prayed about this path and this journey for a year and a half; it was indeed where I was meant to be. By the second semester of the first year however, the path became challenging as I once again found myself single, far from home, with little time to spend with my friends, even less time to make new friends, and no time for sufficient rest. I struggled. I knew God had guided me here, and my family continued to remind me and guide me as well.

The only thing that pulled me through the first two years of medical school was my faith that God had placed me there for a reason, and the support of my family. I cannot attribute much of anything to myself in this time; any strength I pulled from within was one hundred percent a work of God, and the strength I received from my family and friends was a gift from God. I am truly blessed.

I had to continuously remind myself that I had prayed about this path, there was no way God would let me fall. But why did I lose that love and get my heart broken just short of a year after receiving God's message that he heals the brokenhearted? Why did I find myself alone, drowning, using every piece of my being, and every ounce of my faith to keep focused on school?

Although I did not know the answer to this question, God once again showed me He had not forgotten about me. Having just been crying on the phone to my good friend about how much pain I was experiencing with the break up, I pulled myself together enough to walk into a coffee shop to study. After about an hour or two of studying, the man next to me began talking to me about God.

He started quoting the Bible with verses of love. He told me that although he saw a heart full of compassion, he also saw a lot of "unforgiveness" in my heart. What an amazing way to describe the feelings I had been feeling toward my former love, and another close relationship in my life. It rang so true with me and I began to think about it more thereafter.

I never thought of myself as unforgiving. In fact, I always thought I was too quick to forgive, allowing others to "get away" with too much, and sometimes felt taken advantaged. The man at the coffee shop then grabbed my hand and said "Also, God wants you to know He loves you."

Once again, I felt this with every piece of my body and I cried. The man prayed with me and then left. Although I had been questioning why God told me that He healed the brokenhearted, yet broke my heart shortly thereafter, I knew He wanted me in school. His message solidified the fact that He was with me wherever I was, and I could continue to trust in His path for me. But when you're in the midst of a storm, this is easier said than done.

In the middle of the first semester in my second year, six months after my encounter with the man in the coffee shop, I was struggling even more. I was still tormented by my broken heart, and somehow still missing the man who broke it. This struggle was compounded by feelings of shame from the emotional interactions I had intermittently engaged myself in with him in my effort to protect my well-being and my path, and feelings of shame that I was not strong enough to move on from him on my own. I never however, found shame in loving him. But why was this particular break up so difficult for me?

I had never needed a man in the past. Maybe experiencing a connection like that made me realize what I was missing, and almost needing, in my life.

In addition to this struggle, the continued distress of feeling isolated while sitting at my desk twelve to fifteen hours a day, studying, with little time to spend with the few friends I had, and no time to meet new people, created the perfect emotional storm and provided me no chance to move on from my broken heart. I'm a people-person; my isolation was exacerbating every painful thought and feeling I had, and it began to affect me physically. One weekend I found myself waking up in the middle of the night because I had developed a painful rash.

I joked it was bed bugs to freak out my cousin (my roommate at the time) who also happened to share my fear of lice and bugs, but there were no bed bugs to be found. I lost my appetite at one point and was approached about this. A few months later, I even began losing my hair; pulling out clumps any time I brushed my hand through it. I was not enjoying this path, this path I had prayed so long to find; it was lonely, painful, stressful, and even with all of my signs, I felt abandoned by God.

I began to ask for another sign. I figured if God had sent one, I must have missed it. So, I asked again, but this time I called on my grandfather asking him "for a sign that I was on the right path." Not too many days later, it may have even been the next day, I went to a store for wall decorations. A store I never find myself shopping at, for things I never find myself shopping for. I came across a framed poem that looked oddly familiar. It was old but I was attracted to it. I recognized it as something that had been hanging in my grandparent's basement when my grandfather was alive.

I had never seen it elsewhere, and questioned if it were somehow the exact same one. I thought it was odd that I came across it but having been at the store for wall décor, I tried to put it down as it was not aesthetically pleasing. Something prevented me from doing so and I ended up taking it home with me. When I got home, I pulled it out and read the poem in its entirety:

The Footprints of God

In deepest sleep one night I dreamed

That on the beach I walked.

God was by my side each step

And quietly we talked.

Then on the sky my life was flashed;

The visions all serene.

Two sets of footprints in the sand

Were there in every scene.

But then I noticed in some scenes

Of suffering, pain and strife...

Just a single set of footprints

At the worst times of my life.

"God...you said you'd stay by my side

In good times and in bad...

Why then did you leave my side

Each time my life was sad?"

"My precious child," God answered

"When your life had pain, I knew.

The single set of footprints

Were the times I carried you."

- Kent Brown 1984

I once again found myself in tears, something that had become more of a daily occurrence these days; but this time, they were tears of hope and love. I immediately knew this was my sign. I called my sister, the creator of this book, and read her the poem. Hearing her tears on the other line further confirmed this sign. She felt the strength of the message to the same extent I did, no hesitation.

Although the path can still be difficult, and I had a strong faith before, this strengthened my faith even more. I knew God heard me and I knew He would get me through the pain. He wanted me on this path and He is keeping me on this path. He has blessed me with an amazing family who has never made me feel like a burden, and friends who remain my friends even if I uncharacteristically break plans with them due to the stress of school. Although I still need to read this poem and remind myself of God's love, I know now more than ever that "I can do all things through Christ who strengthens me" – Philippians 4:13.

I sit here one year later, September 6th, 2017, having completed my first set of board exams, beginning my third year of medical school and first year of rotations, with excitement and faith that there is no other place I should be. Interacting with patients and physicians in my first two rotations has reignited my personality and my love for life and the path I am on. Also, faith that I will find love again, a love that will build me up, and welcome and embrace all the love I have to share.

Although I have no idea where my path will lead me and I have never been without a conscious goal or a plan, I am following my heart and learning to become one with it and one with others. Knowing that God has full control of my life, I decide every day to leave it up to Him. I am climbing this mountain of life, and although it could be much easier and faster to drive through the tunnel beneath, it would never provide me the view of God's world from the mountain top.

Climbing mountains are tough and sometimes you question what you've put yourself through, but remembering to experience the beauty makes it worth every step. I am enjoying this path where God has me today and I am excited to find out where He leads me later.

A Walk with a Stranger

By: Allison Alexander

I have been to five continents and more cities than I can count. As I sit here with a glass of wine and my dusty journals from those adventures, I am noticing a beautiful pattern. What sticks out the most in my memory and from the pages of my old journals is not the amazing sites I've been to, but the people I've met on my travels. For me, one of the biggest miracles was being hundreds of thousands of miles away from "home" and seeing how God put perfect strangers in my path at the perfect time.

We come into contact with strangers every day. Maybe someone opens the door for you, maybe it's a smile, or maybe just a glance. In our fast-paced lives, we might not even notice. World travel helps put things in perspective. It slows things down. God is doing little things for us every day, but if we don't slow down to notice, we might get lost. We might miss a beautiful connection with a stranger at the perfect time.

I am certainly not the most well-traveled, but I have been fortunate enough to have taken a few worldly adventures so far. I have found that while traveling with friends is most enjoyable, traveling solo offers a unique opportunity to see and do things you might not have otherwise done.

While studying abroad in Australia, I took a solo trip to Sydney to do some exploring. It was a rainy November day, and I was on a quest to see the Sydney Harbour Bridge. I took the ferry to Watson Bay, and as soon as I got off, the rain started pouring down. As I walked toward the bay, I was getting more and more soaked. I stopped by a local pub to ask where I could buy an umbrella. The bartender walked over to the "lost and found," grabbed an umbrella and gave it to me. I was so moved by his creative generosity.

The rain had finally subsided, and while I knew I was getting close to the bridge, I found myself walking in circles on the side streets searching for the not-so-obvious pedestrian access sign. When I passed a young man for the third time, I couldn't help but wonder if we were both lost. We made eye contact and I asked him if he was looking for the access to the bridge. When I found out he was also lost, I felt an immediate sense of comfort in knowing I wasn't alone in this quest.

We joined forces and finally found the bridge entrance. We ended up walking across the entire bridge together. Turns out he was from Germany and also on a solo holiday. Some 12 years later, I still remember that walk with that man. We had an excellent conversation—the kind where you forget about time. It was effortless, it flowed, it was interesting, but what's fascinating is that now I can't tell you one thing we talked about.

When we got to the end of the bridge we thanked each other for the walk and parted ways, as if we both knew we would never see each other again but we were meant to walk the Sydney Harbour Bridge together that day. As I walked back to my hostel to dry off, it occurred to me that I didn't even know his name. We walked for over a mile together and we never exchanged names.

As I reflect, I can't help but be blown away by the circumstances of that day. It was pouring rain with no convenient store in sight to buy an umbrella, and I happened to pick a pub to stop in that happened to have a cheery bartender, who happened to find a spare umbrella in the "lost and found" bin. I was halfway across the world from anything that resembled "home."

In a city of over 5 million people, I happened to cross paths with another international traveler, who was also lost, and we happened to find the bridge entrance together. Even though I don't remember what we talked about that day, I remember how I felt. I remember that I didn't feel alone anymore in a huge city. I remember thinking what a beautiful blessing it was that our paths crossed at that very moment.

I recently read a book with a phrase that struck me in an "ah-ha" sort of way... "Coincidences are just God's way of staying incognito!" That couldn't be more true! It was no coincidence that I picked the one pub that had an umbrella. It was no coincidence that my nameless stranger-friend and I crossed paths at that very moment and had a beautiful walk across the Sydney Harbour Bridge. God put those people there for me and me for them.

In today's high-tech society we have smartphones, iPads, tablets, and fancy widgets at our fingertips 24/7. What if I had a smartphone that day walking across that bridge? Would I have even been lost? Would my Google Maps just have taken me directly to the bridge entrance? Would my head have been down looking at directions, instead of up so that I would have never made eye contact with my nameless stranger-friend? Would we have just passed each other? What if that beautiful walk and conversation never happened? Sure, I would have remembered going to see the Sydney Harbour Bridge, but it would have been just another walk.

These kinds of *miracles* have happened to me more times than I can remember during my travels. When I was in Japan with my friend Shannon, we spent a few days in Tokyo. We got off the train in search of our capsule hotel, but our map was confusing as were the Japanese signs. We were walking for a while when we passed a man walking in the opposite direction. While he didn't speak any English, he must have sensed that we were lost and he stopped to help. He looked at our map as we pointed to where we wanted to be.

This kind Japanese gentleman proceeded to guide us to our hotel, which was at least a 10-minute walk in the opposite direction he was originally going. We were walking in a city of over 13 million people ... and happened to pass a man that was willing to walk 10 minutes out of his way to make sure we got to our hotel. As we walked into our hotel, my heart was overflowing with gratitude for that man's kindness.

The universe and God work in mysterious but more importantly miraculous ways. God has a way of putting the most perfect people in our paths at the most perfect time ... we just need to keep our eyes open and our heads up in order to see them!

Japanese Butterflies

By: Shannon Robak

The sound of the rain. The intricate patterns of flowers. The steam from my coffee. I didn't know these would be some of my favorite memories from Japan that I would treasure most. In September 2014, I signed a year-long contract to teach English to Japanese students - I thought it was a great opportunity to work and travel the world at the same time. I didn't really know what to expect though as I hadn't done any research about the Japanese culture. The little I did know was that they were known for their sushi, sumo wrestling, and the infamous Mt. Fuji. As I soon found out though, it would be the butterflies that would impact me the most.

Soon after arriving in Japan, I realized how long a year in this country was actually going to be. The Japanese culture is the most unique culture I have yet to experience. The Japanese people are without question some of the most polite people in the world, but I quickly learned that it isn't easy for foreigners to become immersed into their culture - something I definitely struggled with. Miscommunications and the language barrier were sometimes too much for me to handle. I usually thrive on building personal connections with others, but the Japanese people are very private, so creating strong relationships with them was a challenge. That being said, God provided me many blessings throughout the year that were constant reminders that He was with me.

For my year-long teaching assignment, I originally wanted to be in Tokyo (of course!), but we didn't have a choice on where we were placed. I was assigned to a small town called Kamisu, about an hour and a half northeast of Tokyo. After my first few weeks I realized how blessed I was to have been placed in Kamisu. For one, I was given my own car. Imagine that! They gave me a car in Japan! Had I been placed in Tokyo, I would have been taking trains to and from work, which would have consisted of train changes and a commute of at least 40 minutes. In Kamisu, not only did I have a three-minute commute with my own car, I had the freedom to explore more of Japan at my own pace—not to mention the adventure that came along with the car itself.

The Japanese drive on the opposite side of the road, which, of course, I was not used to. In my first week of driving, I sideswiped a car's side mirror and drove right through all of the stop signs. In my defense, I couldn't read Japanese and the stop signs actually look like yield signs. I mean, what would you do in that situation?!

The studio apartment where I lived couldn't have been more perfect for many reasons. It was small, cozy, and had the best shower in all of Asia. That's not an exaggeration! There was a deadbolt on the front door (which made me feel extra safe) and a patio door allowed a fresh breeze to fill the space. And, BONUS! The apartment came with a rice cooker! What more could I possibly ask for? This studio apartment was a huge blessing and it became my sanctuary.

My apartment was located within walking distance of the local grocery store, a sushi restaurant, and the neighborhood park where I watched the sunset every weekend without fail. Even when it was rainy, cloudy, and I couldn't see the sun, I still went. I also found a Catholic Church that was just a few blocks away from my apartment. In a country where the two main religions are Shinto and Buddhism, what were the odds that this Catholic Church would be located just down the road from me? To be honest, with the way things were going, I wasn't really too surprised.

The neighborhood *Izakaya* (Japanese pub) that I often visited is still my favorite bar in the entire world (again, not an exaggeration). It had such a warm, welcoming atmosphere and the owners treated me as if they had known me for years. On one of my many visits to the bathroom, I noticed a decorative plaque on the wall. Once I looked a little bit closer I saw that it was from Wisconsin - my home state! Clearly this was a sign from God letting me know I was exactly where I was meant to be.

I tell you all of these things to give you a better picture of just how many blessings God bestowed upon me throughout the year. It was obvious to me that I was exactly where God wanted me to be, but still, living there wasn't easy. To be honest, my year in Japan was extremely difficult and at times I felt as though I were living in a year-long meditation course. Don't get me wrong, I loved Japan and the people, but living there for a year was no cake walk!

I arrived in Japan off the heels of living in Nepal, a place where I had a strong emotional connection with the family I was living with and the children I was teaching. There weren't many days that went by that my heart wasn't bursting with joy. However, the Japanese have a more structured way of life and teaching didn't fulfill me as much as it had in Nepal. I felt isolated and experienced a loneliness I had never felt before. A new challenge awaited me here: I was going to need to search deeper within on this part of my journey.

Six mornings a week, no matter how I was feeling or how cold it was outside, I forced myself to get up and go for a morning run. It was one of the only ways I could keep from completely losing my mind.

One of the reasons that I looked forward to my runs was because of the pond that was on my route. It was quiet, peaceful, and I always felt much closer to God while running here. When the famous Japanese cherry blossoms bloomed in the spring, it made my runs even more beautiful.

It wasn't until the second half of the year that I really started to notice the butterflies on my morning runs. They started to make their presence very known, to the point that it was impossible for me not to notice them. The butterflies started flying directly in front of me, as if they had been awaiting my arrival. This became a daily occurrence. I couldn't believe it! And if they weren't escorting me down the path, they were flying circles around me. There were many times that a butterfly came out of nowhere and flew so close to my face that it actually scared me. They were practically grazing my skin!

God made it very obvious that these butterflies weren't just a coincidence. I knew for certain that they were God and His angels reminding me they were constantly with me and watching over me. I felt a tremendous amount of peace and joy in knowing I was protected and God was going to help me get through the year. He was making it very clear!

The butterflies weren't only with me on my runs though. It seemed they were truly following me! Even while driving, they would fly directly in front of my window - I'd almost hit them! I'm surprised that I didn't ever find one sitting next to me in my passenger seat.

Another place I enjoyed hanging out was the library. It was located directly across the street from the school where I taught English classes - another blessing. During my breaks I would walk across the street to sit outside on one of the benches and enjoy the fresh air.

I always found myself sitting on the same bench, which grew to be my favorite. Placed beneath a beautiful tree, the bench offered a relaxing spot to listen to the leaves rustling in the wind; and in a country where silence is considered "golden," I really learned to appreciate the sounds of life. Most importantly for me, this bench was one of the many places where I spent a lot of time praying.

I often prayed that God would help get me through the year without completely losing my sanity. My faith was definitely being tested and at the same time was being strengthened in a way that was new to me. As hard as it was to understand certain things while I was experiencing them, I knew that God could hear my prayers.

It wasn't long before I began to notice the butterflies on the bench, too.

They would fly in the tree above, reassuring me again that I wasn't alone. As my time in Japan drew to an end, the butterflies became even more noticeable - it was like they were now actually trying to slap me across the face!

During one of my breaks from teaching, I was laying on my bench, praying as usual. Before I knew it, a butterfly landed on my knee...and it didn't leave! A man walked right past me, which I thought would for sure scare the butterfly away, but it didn't budge. It was a good 30 seconds before the butterfly finally fluttered away, only to return moments later. I couldn't believe it. Not once, but twice it landed directly on me! Clearly this butterfly was a Heavenly messenger. Tears slowly rolled down my cheeks as I forced myself to get up and head back to class. Moments like this are what brought me an unexplainable peace and joy for which I am forever grateful.

I couldn't believe that my last day of teaching had finally come. This in itself was nothing short of a miracle. It had been a very emotional day and I just wanted a little time to myself, so I decided to pay my bench one final visit. As I was sitting there reflecting on the past year, I had this overpowering feeling that at that moment, someone was sitting on that bench with me. Not only that, my gut was telling me that someone had been sitting with me on that bench for the entire year. Sure enough, at that exact moment, a butterfly began circling around me.

As I got up to return to class, I had a strong urge to look back at the bench. As I turned around for one last glimpse of my favorite bench, I was overcome with emotion. The bench, empty to the naked eye, had in fact been occupied by God and His angels the entire year.

At the moment of acknowledging this in my heart, the same butterfly, as if on cue, landed on my bench. At this point, I pretty much lost it. If there were any passersby, I'm sure they were wondering why this foreign girl was standing, staring at a bench, and crying. It was well over a minute that the butterfly was perched on the bench, just watching me. I even had time to get out my camera and take its picture. I stood there waiting for the butterfly to leave but it never did. Reluctantly and with a grateful heart, I was finally the one who had to turn away.

As if I hadn't already had the perfect last day, it was about to get even better. Every September, my small town, Kamisu, holds the country's biggest *Yosakoi* (Japanese dance) festival. Japanese dance groups from around the country participate, and what are the odds that it was held in the local park where I had watched the sunset every weekend for the past year?! Pretty darn cool!

I went to the festival that Saturday night to celebrate the end of my time in

Japan, just expecting to have a few beers and watch some dancing. I never could have imagined the great celebration God had waiting for me. The park that I had visited almost every day for an entire year was now filled with thousands of Japanese from around the country. It seemed that everyone had come just to celebrate and wish me a safe journey. How kind of them!

The best part of the night was the fireworks. Not only did it feel like the entire Japanese population was there celebrating with me, it seemed that the angels in Heaven were also throwing me a huge party. God's timing for these fireworks could not have been more perfect. As I watched the dance groups with the fireworks booming overhead, I felt like the most blessed person on this entire planet. God was surely alive this night and I did my best to soak up every minute of it!

There were many times throughout the year that I honestly didn't know if I was going to make it. But during my lowest moments, God was right there with me. This "year-long meditation course" strengthened my relationship and faith in God in ways I never could have imagined possible. If I had to re-live that year, even knowing what I know now, I would. I now better understand that God's plan is absolutely perfect and His perspective is much greater than ours. I have also learned that spending time with Him is when I am able to find the most peace, joy, and meaning from life.

God travels with us wherever we go. No matter our destination, He's already one step ahead with great plans that await us. The butterflies even followed me to Nepal. But that story is for another time...

A Note About
"Miracle Moments in Travel"

All of the proceeds from this book will go towards a cultural exchange program that provides opportunities for Nepali youth to experience American culture. To learn more about the children who will benefit from this program, you can read the first book they published entitled "Our Earthquake Experience," which describes their firsthand experiences during the earthquake that hit Nepal in April of 2015.

To make a contribution to our education fund for the children of Nepal, please visit our website at www.WhyNotNowMissions.org or send us an email at WhyNotNowMissions@gmail.com. If you have any questions or general inquiries, we would love to hear from you.

Additional copies of this book and "Our Earthquake Experience" can be purchased on Amazon.

Thank you!

About the Author

Over the years, Shannon Robak has been blessed with the opportunity to travel throughout different regions of the world. Though the sights of a new place are beautiful and full of adventure, what strikes her the most is her realization of how perfect God's plan is. She is humbled by how much God has taken care of her and amazed at how God chooses to reveal Himself along her life journey.

She loves to hear other people's travel experiences and could talk about God, angels, and divine intervention for hours. She currently resides in Milwaukee, Wisconsin where she enjoys reading, running, and eating a lot of rice!

Front Cover Photo : Cerro de la Cruz, Antigua, Guatemala

Back Cover Photo: Rooftop in Bagdol, Nepal

www.ingramcontent.com/pod-product-compliance
Lightning Source LLC
Chambersburg PA
CBHW071020040426
42443CB00007B/862